Acknowledgements

I'd like to thank the following for making my life enjoyable & worthwhile.

Helena McCaffery, Kevin O'Flanagan , Cissy O'Flanagan, Teresa O'Flanagan, Moira O'Flanagan, Brian O'Flanagan, Oliver O'Flanagan, Aine O'Flanagan, Liam O'Flanagan, Aileen O'Flanagan, Colm O'Flanagan, Kevin O'Flanagan, Rory O'Flanagan, Theresa O'Flanagan, Ciaran O'Flanagan Darragh O'Flanagan, Ferga O'Flanagan, Ruadhan O'Flanagan, Ciara O'Flanagan Desmond O'Flanagan,Eileen O'Flanagan, Anne O'Flanagan, Roseleen O'Flanagan, Sean O'Flanagan, Mary O'Flanagan, Susan O'Flanagan,Joe Maher, Annie Maher, Tommy Maher Paul Maher, Angela Maher, John Maher, Margaret Maher, Gerry Bailey, Sean Bailey, Gerard Bailey, Rory Bailey, Brendan Bailey, Canon Hickey, Miss Lavin, Brother Loftus, Master O'Keefe, Brother Perkins, Leo McCaffrey, Nell McCaffrey, Frank Murray, Ferga McGratten Paul Scully, Declan Collinge, Laurance Corrigan, Des McDonald, Shay McCarthy, Phyllis Hall Joan Sherry, Lilly Hennesy, Mary Courtney, Evelyn Buckley, Angela Courtney, Tony Cullen, Anne Leonard, John Field, Rory Furlong, Colin Beggan, Jack Walsh, Eamon Drummond, Pat Lennon, Brush Shiels, Mary Lennon, Phillip Lynott, Gary Moore, Noel Bridgeman, Bernard Cheevers, Brian Downey, Smiley Bolger Jon Hodges, Rita Fagan, Eilish Comerford, Jo Kennedy, Eadaoin Ni Clearaigh, John Gallagher, Michael Conaghan ,Antoinette Deegan, Eric Byrne, Paul Hand, Vincent Stapleton, Maurice Coen, Michelle Heery, Robert Foley, Raymond Lambert, Mary Waddell, Fintan Connolly, Joan Stapleton, Monica Lupton,Vincent Jackson, Gerry Gill, Aengus O'Snodaigh, Brid Smith, Tina McVeigh, Robert Ballagh, Tommy Smith, Criona Ni Dalaigh, Aisling Ni Dalaigh, Michael MacDonnacha, Alan Farrell, David McFarlane, Clifton Collins, Jen Bowen, Michelle Rutledge, Brian O'Connor, Catherine Byrne, Cathy Byrne, Zane Cilova, Seosamh O'Broin, Cathy Scuffil, Raymond McGovern, Rebecca Rolfe, Helen Scott, Rita Sutton, Desmond Fennell, John Robb, Raymond Crotty, Tom Barrington, David Pierpoint, Susan Denham, Frank Connolly, Richard Roche,Ray Williams,, Angela Rolfe, Danny Morrison, Tommy Graham,Tom Stokes Frank Allen, Tomas Gleeson, Brendan O'Neill, Niamh Kavanagh, Derick Warfield, Gerry Adams, Anthony Coughlin, Tom Hartley, Sean Dublin Bay Loftus, Fr. Mick O'Connor, George Boyle,Gwen Doyle, Fr. Sean Healy, Fiach MacConghail, Janice & Billy, Eileen O'Meara, Liam O'Meara, Patricia Tierney, Anne Marie O'Brien, Edmund Penrose, Finbar Cullen, Terry O'Neill, Mo Alam, Neville Keery, Padraig Yeates, May McGiolla, Thomas McGiolla ,Bruce, Philips, Manus O'Riordan, Ruan O'Donnell, Desmond Egan, Bob Shakeshaft, Violet Balfe, Vawn Corrigan, Brendan Kenny, Rosemarie Rowley, Margaret Boles, Phill Conway, James Conway, Eithne Cavanagh, Mary Guckian, Ciara Scott, Maria Guinan, Niall Bergin, Rose Dugdale Muriel McAuley, Vincent McManus, Nial Ring, Treasa Quinn, Owen Curran, Martin Mansergh, Una O'Callanain, Ruairi.McGinley, Maire Devine, Michael D. Higgins, Rebecca Moynihan,,Carmel McCartney, Shannon Murray,Paddy Murray, Christine Broe, Aoife Hannon, Catherine Ardagh, John Houlihan,, John Lee, Jean O'Brien, Peter Byrne, Eilish Byrne, Alison Maddock, Damien Maddock, Brendan Quinn, Roseanne Farrell, Sinead Clancy, Chris Byne, Joe Guinan, Samantha McCoombe, Carmel Sammon, Margaret Hyland, Maeve McDonald,Clinton McDonald, Mary McAleese, Francis Devine, Bruce Phillips, Leo Johnson, Gerry O'Donohgue, and Sinead Murphy.

The Importance Of Fruit

The Importance of Fruit

First Published 2018

ISBN 9781901596267

Riposte Books

msriposte@gmail.com

28 Emmet Road Kilmainham Dublin 8

**Printed by Digital Print Dynamics.
Ballycoolin, Dublin 11**

and

**Bound by Trinity Book-binding
Co. Dublin**

"The next day as they were leaving Bethany, Jesus was hungry. Seeing in the distance a fig tree in leaf, he went to find out if it had any fruit. When he reached it, he found nothing but leaves, because it was not the season for figs. Then he said to the tree, "May no one ever eat fruit from you again". And his disciples heard him say it. The following morning, as they went along, they saw the fig tree withered from the roots."

Matthew 21:19- Mark 11:14

Kevin O'Flanagan and Cissy Maher get married in September 1947.
Roseleen O'Fanagan, Michael O'Flanagan, Ann O'Flanagan Sean
O'Flanagan Hannah Parkinson Sara Burke, John Maher. John Maher,
Annie Maher, Joe Maher, Tommy Maher, Ellen Burke,

Kevin and Cissy cut the cake 1947   Michael, Moira and Brian 1953

First Memories

Bunting Road 1953

On the 10th of March 1953 I was out playing football with my two friends Pat Lennon and Keith Conroy. We were playing with a group of other children on the grass verge outside my house at 112 Bunting Road. I was four and a half years old. It was quite common for young children to be allowed out to play on the footpath and even on the road in those days, because traffic was very scarce and motorists traveled at much slower speeds and often came across children playing football in the middle of the road. So on this occasion there were about eight children gathered together outside my house when a car pulled up and stopped. It was then that my friends Pat and Keith who were slightly older than me, explained to me why the car was there. It was a hearse which had come to collect my mother who, unknown to me, had died the previous evening. This sudden news had a profound effect on me and altered the rest of my life. The following days were filled with tears, temper-tantrums and unanswerable questions. My mum was a mere thirty-three years old when she died and my father who was the exact same age, now had three young children to cope with and I was clearly going to be the least co-operative. Doubtless for me, this has become the habit of a lifetime. Over the years I have encountered many shocks and surprises and I have learned to be prepared for the unexpected but the shock of losing my mum at such an early age has never faded from my memory

Kevin O'Flanagan. Michael, Cissy O'Flanagan, and Granny O'Flanagan at Sunday tea on Emmet Road 1949

Joe and Annie Maher and Tommy and Cissy Maher 1950

Kevin holding Michael, Cissy holding Moira and Joe holding Paul

Cissy Maher

Margaret Maher was called Cissy Maher because she was the only sister in a family of four boys, John, Gerry, Joe and Tommy. Cissy was the daughter of John Maher and Sarah Burke. John worked for the ESB and granny Maher was dealer in the Iveagh market. As I remember granny Maher she wore a very large apron made from a padded quilt with a monster pocket at the front, full of half crowns. She always gave us a half crown for our communion and this was a sizeable sum in the 1950s. As for my mum, my memories of her are necessarily few as she died when I was so young. My earliest memory is of her giving me a slap for tipping over my potty while she was breast feeding my sister Moira. My mum was a very talented dress maker and she made all my clothes including a pair of blue dungarees which survived long after she died. Children's clothes in the 1950s were dull and dreary and she was keen to dress us up and show us off. My mother died of Leukemia and was sick for a year before she died. She spent several periods in hospital presumingly getting blood transfusions. During these periods I was looked after by my cousin Michael who set up a chicken run for me at the end of our back garden on Bunting road. So it was that on one occasion when my mum had just arrived home from hospital on a very windy night, all I was interested in talking to her about was my concern for my favourite hen Wilbur. I was afraid that he would be harmed by the ferocious wind. As time went by my mother spent more and more time in bed and I can clearly remember sitting with my sister Moira at the end of her bed eating our porridge. My final memory of my mum was in the room shortly before she died. The brilliant shine on the red linoleum, the candles lit on the locker and the picture of Pope Pius XII on the wall. When she left us I was four and a half years old, Moira was two and my brother Brian was a mere eleven months old.

Chicken Cullen's Cottage at the top of Bunting Road

Philip Lynott in Mooney's field at the end of Bunting Road 1965

112 Bunting Road 1998

Life on Bunting Road

Bunting road in the 1950s was unusual in that it had a large field (Mooney's field) at one end and a traditional farmer's cottage and chicken run at the other end. The road which was nearly a quarter of a mile long had private purchase houses on both sides. This was at a time when Dublin Corporation were building thousands of council houses for rent in Crumlin, Ballyfermot, Bluebell and Drimnagh and all in close proximity to Walkinstown. Nearly all of the 180 houses on Bunting road had large families many with young children. It was not uncommon for hundreds of children to be out playing on Bunting road in the late fifties and early sixties both in summer and winter. There were no playgrounds in the vicinity, indeed I can't remember if playgrounds had been invented. The children made their own fun with the girls playing piggy beds and the boys playing cowboys and Indians. Many games were also played outside "the powerhouse" at the top of Bunting road where both boys and girls played "broken statues." When the Irish army went to the Congo some the boys swapped their Davey Crockett hats for United Nations blue helmets while others were condemned to play Baluba's. Every girl had her own skipping rope and every boy made his own bow and arrow. Boys made boxcars from butter-boxes with old bicycle wheels and gigs with ball-races from the engines buses as a number of men on Bunting road were mechanics in Dublin Bus. These were also the source of "steelys" large steel balls which were ideal for playing marbles especially along the edge of the road when we played "gulliers." Different games were played when in "season" thus "conkers" was played in the Autumn when the chess-nuts were ripe and ready to be picked and collected often in the Phoenix park. Shops near Bunting road included Kilcullen's on Walkinstown road where loose goods were sold including sugar and flour which was weighed and deposited in brown paper bags. It had all the atmosphere of an old country shop. Perri's beside The Cherry Tree

FL: Stephnie Cummins, Mary Lennon,Vivien McGillcudy, Dymphna McGown Moira O'Flanagan,Angela Maher, Patricia Dwyer, Caraline Harris Anne Gleeson, Anne Brennan, Conor Cummins,Dermot McGillicudy, Sean Judge,John Maher, Paul Maher, Brian O'Flanagan, Michael O'Flanagan, Brendan McCann, Eamon McCann

sold newspapers, crisps and sweets with the added attraction of stocking model aeroplanes and ships which were very popular at that time. There was also Rushes Pork Shop next door to Perri's were you could buy pork pies, sausages and dripping which was universally used for frying in those days. Pork shops were separate and distinct from butchers shops and only sold pork products. At the junction of Walkinstown road and Ballymount Lane was The Monument Creamery where butter was sold loose. Butter was cut out from a large block with butter pats, weighed and sold in grease-proof paper. The butter arrived to the shop in large sturdy wooden butter-boxes which were often subsequently used as furniture in poorer house-holds. The most exciting shop in the area was Desmond's. As you walked into Desmond's you first encountered a bank of glass-topped biscuit boxes which allowed you to view the biscuits inside. The biscuits were sold loose and weighed so that you could buy a quarter pound of lemon creams. Desmond's also sold lucky lumps which were raspberry flavoured lumps of sugar which, if you were lucky had a trupenny bit inside. They also sold Honeybee sweets at two for a farthing. This shop also sold a wide

range of toys including cap guns. These guns held rolls of caps which could be bought as refills and allowed children to run around making loud bangs as they played cowboys and Indians. Shops at the other end of Bunting Road included the ABC stores where the week's groceries could be bought "on the slate." Close-by was Findlaters who did deliveries with delivery boys on specially built bicycles with a large delivery tray on the front of the bike. Unlike other grocery shops, Findlaters also sold stout by the bottle and fortified wines. Nearly everything on sale in those days was weighed and you could buy a quarter of a pound of sausages (ie.. two sausages.) Even eggs were sold loose so it was not uncommon for someone to buy one egg, one rasher and one sausage. Naturally fruit and vegetables were all sold loose and stored in large wooden boxes higgley piggley and seldom washed so that you brought home clay in your shopping bag. There were no plastic bags so everybody brought a shopping bag or basket when they went shopping. Everything was sold from behind the counter and the shop assistant had to be told what you wanted, there was no such thing as self service. When the "Walk-around Stores" were introduced and customers were allowed to pick up the items they wanted, customers were insulted when they were told to place all their chosen items in a wire basket because they thought this was a slight on their honesty.

At the Halfway House there were two other shops, Grealishes and Michael's corner. In Michael's Corner you could buy homemade ice-pops and Grealishes sold a wide rage of items including utensils and

material for baking. Bread, scones and soda cakes were baked sometimes daily in nearly every home in those days. Ice-cream of course was also sold loose and you could order a three-penny wafer or six-penny wafer which was twice as thick. Nearly all shops sold cigarettes and the shopkeepers had no difficulty in selling cigarettes

to children especially if they had a note from their parents. Indeed shopping was never done in bulk and children were constantly running to the shops to buy one or two items scribbled on a note. Children sent to the shop for a batch loaf would often have it half eaten by the time they got home as it was sold unwrapped. However, children sent to the Chemist with a note often carried home mystery items very carefully wrapped in brown paper packages.

The Walkinstown Roundabout.

Michael Cullen (aka "Chicken Cullen" because he kept a chicken run behind his house) lived in a house on the corner of Wilkinstown Cross built by his father in 1865. The house was built where the three townlands of Wilkinstown, Greenhills and Crumlin Common came together. The name Wilkinstwon is on the deeds of most of the houses in Walkinstown and the area's name was only changed when the Bird Flanagan called his house Walkinstown House. This was to distinguish it from Wilkinstown in county Meath. As the new housing estates of Dublin began to swallow up the idyllic countryside in the fifties many new roads were opened up and Wilkinstown Cross (now Walkinstown Cross) on the main road from Dublin to Tallaght at the junction of the Greenhills Rd. and Cromwellsfort Lane became a mega junction with seven roads all meeting together. In 1950, Michael Cullen, 65, refused to sell his home to Dublin Corporation for £1000, despite being served with a compulsory purchase order. Dublin Corporation had built Michael a new house, a bungalow, the first one on the left side of Walkinstown Avenue, a mere thirty yards from his Cottage. However Michael refused to move to this new house, as the Corporation refused to grant him freehold on the new property and demanded one shilling per year in rent. As a result a twenty-one year battle ensued and Mr. Cullen became famous nationally and locally. Dublin Corporation then built a road system around the

Cullen house, effectively marooning Mr Cullen in the middle of what is the modern day Walkinstown roundabout, Mysteriously and without notice in 1971, Mr. Cullen, moved his belongings to the new house across the road. The Corporation immediately demolished the old Cottage. Mr. Cullen lived until 1980 dying at the age of 95.

The 50B bus which had it's terminus at Chicken Cullen's Cottage where I got off the bus every evening after work in the 1960s

Desmonds shop which was adjacent to Chicken Cullen's cottage can be seen in this photo. The bus conductor is having a smoke and sharing a light with a local woman at the bus terminus.

Early Days at School

I started school in The National School on St. Agnes' Road Crumlin in 1953. I was in Miss Lavin's Class which comprised Low babies, High babies and First Class. There was 85 in the class. Miss Lavin used to brighten up the room with props from the local Chemist shops, pop-up figures which she put on the window sills. She always had two pound of raisins on her desk and she would give the best behaved and best performing children a handful of raisins to encourage effort among her students. She lived in a house just opposite the school and she grew potatoes in her front garden. On one occasion she gave me a shilling for picking the potatoes. The toilets were in an out-house at back of the school and they often froze up in winter. In 1956 during the Hungarian revolution many Hungarians came to Ireland fleeing from the Communists and four Hungarian children joined our class in the National School. They all brought towels and soap to school with them every day. There was just one large sink in the school and it was always full to the top with dirty water. Students tried to push one and other into the sink. A very large tree in front of the school had been cut down leaving a giant stump in the middle of the yard. Mr. Cassidy told the children to bring in nails which they then spent the lunch periods hammering the nails into the stump. Eventually it was worn away by this activity. Mr. Cassidy also had us all bring in old newspapers to make fáinní or rings to keep the fire going and to heat the class room. Mr. Cassidy had 2nd,3rd and 4th classes in the one room. He delegated some of the older students to check the spellings of the younger students. I left for Drimnagh Castle after 2nd class.

My Dad

Born in May 1920 the second son of my grandfather Michael O'Flanagan, Kevin O'Flanagn lived all his life in shadow of his father. My grandfather was the General Secretary of the Printers' Union from 1913 until 1920, the year my father was born. In that same year his uncle Tommy helped to burn down The Custom House and spent the subsequent year in Kilmainham Gaol. My dad's aunt Ellen was a school teacher who had fought in The GPO in 1916. So it was that in a quiet and non-flamboyant way he knew that he was a member of no mean family. The pride of his life was his own family of twelve children. His twelve children born to two wives Cissy Maher and Teresa Leavey were the source of all his happiness and the catalyst to his every endeavour. The death of my mother in 1953 was a major blow to my dad leaving him as it did with three young children under five. In those days it was quite common for husbands to die young and the widows struggled along to raise their children with what help they could get from family and friends. But a man left with three young children would have no where to turn. I have never doubted that my father loved me and I have often been told that I was his blue-eyed boy yet it was a shock that as a five years old he sat me down and asked me how I would feel about going into an orphanage. The amazing thing about this story is that my father accepted a firm "No" from a five year old. Over the following twenty-seven years until his death in 1980 I learned much and gained wisdom from watching my father and how he lived his life. He loved the outdoors and brought the family camping and fishing and touring throughout the country showing us the rivers and mountains from Ben Bulben to Killarney from Vinegar Hill to the hills of Donegal. He knew the best places to fish both on rivers and in the sea. He collected cockles and dug for bait at Sandymount strand and he loved to swim in the sea. It was an article of faith with him that you should have your own transport probably arising from the fact that he worked night-work in both The Irish Press and the Irish Times for most of his life. He had numerous cars over the years from his first Ford Anglia to his last Baby Fiat. Indeed he spent much of his free time fixing punctures and rooting around under the bonnet of various different cars. But his ability to go where no public transport existed was central to his belief as to how life could best be enjoyed. He strongly believed that the remedies to common illnesses could always be found in the locality where the illness occurred. This prompted him to bring us all collecting blackberries, other wild berries and nuts, mushrooms and all kinds of shellfish. He taught me how to ground fish in the sea and use spinners in the rivers. He knew how to cook cockles and dress crabs. He was an excellent Chess player and he loved to play a wide range of tunes on his Piccolo. He was "Father of the Chapel" for many years in both The Irish Press and the Irish Times. As a compositor he used both Linotype and Monotype setting methods and was among the first to use the new technology of computerised composition. However, his main skill was as a Gaelic reader, correcting errors in the Irish articles submitted to the newspapers for publication. He was a fluent Irish speaker and encouraged the whole family to use the couple of focal throughout the day within the household. He loved the old Irish airs which he could play on his violin, his favourite among them was An Chúilfhionn. He took his politics from his uncle and aunt who had fought in the struggle for Irish Independence. He sided with the Provisional's during the troubles. He died in 1980 just weeks before the first the Hunger Strike. The oration at his grave was given by Charlie McGlade who had been a close friend of my Grandfather from the time they had worked together in Cahill's Printing Company as far back as the 1940s. My dad sent this postcard to our family from Lourdes in September 1980 and it arrived at our house just in time for the morning of his funeral.

Michael O'Flanagan

My Grandfather Michael O'Flanagan, Myself & My Dad Kevin O'Flanagan

Michael O'Flanagan was my grandfather. He was born in Co. Tyrone in 1880. He was a compositor. In 1901 he was living with his father and mother in Dominick street along with his brothers John, Joe, Tommy, and Francis and with his sisters Ellen Sarah and Kathleen.. In 1911 he was living with his newly wed wife Aine in Bride Street. They had five children Dessie, Eileen, Kevin, Sean and Ann. By 1913 he was the General secretary of the Dublin Typographical Provident Society, the Printers Union. He is reputed to have gone down to the docks with a posse wielding a gun to warn off blacklegs during the Great Lockout. In 1916 he threatened the Editor of the Irish Independent that he would call out the printers on strike from their newspaper if they did not modify their scurrilous editorials on the Easter Rising. His sister Ellen had fought in the Four Courts. His brother Tommy spent a year in Kilmainham Gaol for burning down the Custom House. He was fluent Irish speaker and he gave Irish lessons to the children of Keogh's square in the 1920s at a penny a lesson. He allowed the headquarters of the Union at 35 Lr. Gardiner

Ellen O'Flanagan Granny O'Flanagan Aunt Eileen and Uncle Dessie.

Street to be used as the HQ of Dublin Battalion of the IRA during the War of Independence. He was sacked from his position as General Secretary of the Union in 1920 for using Union funds to assist IRA volunteers on the run to flee the country. He returned to work as a compositor in Cahill's where he was Father of the Chapel for many years. He died in 1948 a few months before I was born.

Michael O'Flanagan's testimonial and a letter he wrote to the Women's Union 1919

Drimnagh Castle

I took up my place in Drimnagh Castle at nine years of age in 1957. My first teacher there was Brother Loftus which was ironic as the most famous person ever to own the castle was Adam Loftus who became the Lord Chancllor of Ireland in 1619. Brother Loftus was far from being the worst Christian brother ever to teach in Drimnagh Castle. Although fond of using the leather he was an excellent teacher and had several tricks to engage the pupils. I remember when it snowed he brought the class out to play snowballs behind the Castle on the edge of the moat. Then again on most Friday afternoons he would sit up on the front desk and read aloud chapters from Alice in Wonderland and from Treasure Island. When the Primary school opened first in Drimnagh Castle in 1957 the classes were held in the old Castle itself while the brand new school was being built in the surrounding grounds belonging to the Castle. I was in third class and my classroom was in the stables of the castle while second class was held in the coach-house across the yard. We had to cross the moat via the redundant drawbridge to enter the castle. We never saw the inside of the dungeon but we were often brought up to the main hall of the castle for singing lessons by Brother Loftus. I chugged across a piece of waste ground behind

Walkinstown Church as a short cut to the Castle four times a day on my way to school all the way from Bunting Road. I remember being told that we were allowed home for lunch because that had been the habit during the war when the Gas supply was only turned on for a couple of hours in the middle of the day to save coal. I still suspect it was to allow the Christian Brothers go to their lunch in the Monastery. In 1958 we all moved into the new school. The contrast between the conditions of the castle stables and the coach-house and

the polished floors of the new school was quite mind-blowing. Most amazing was the huge school hall which had a full size stage. This, and the large influx of new students to fill all those extra class rooms allowed the teachers to set up drama groups and choirs and put on shows and plays. The whole thing caused a spectacular outburst of enthusiasm Mr first teacher in the new school was Mr.O'Keefe. He prepared our class for Confirmation. We made our confirmation in St. Agnes's church in Crumlin because while the new church in Walkinstown was now complete it had not achieved parish status. So it was that our fourth class was the first class in Drimnagh Castle to have our group confirmation photograph taken on the steps of the new school. Here I can be seen as always front and centre and third from the left wearing my Castle cap and Dickie bow. There is little to report of my fifth and sixth years in Drimnagh castle primary school beyond that I passed my Primary Cert. with little distinction and thus automatically qualified to enter Drimnagh Castle secondary school. Boys from other schools had to do an entrance exam. I entered the secondary in September 1960 and was placed in 1B. The following year I was dropped to 2C because I wasn't keeping up with the other boys but at least I didn't land in 2D. Drimnagh Castle secondary was a very strict school and indiscipline could get you expelled very quickly. Many boys left the school because the discipline was too strict and because academic achievement was required from all students. Mr. Dunleavey taught us Latin and mathematics. I made a fair fist of the mathematics but Latin was beyond me. Mr. Bowe taught us English and Geography. He awakened a genuine interest in me in Poetry which served me well to this day. Geography was a different matter. Most boys had a standard school atlas. I didn't. My father was reluctant to buy me one because we had a Reader's Digest Atlas at home. This was an enormous book which weighed several pounds. Mr. Bowe wasn't impressed and doubted that the book existed. After several daily disputes he ordered me to yoke up the ass and cart and bring the book into school. Eventually I brought the atlas in and a whole

Brother Perkins   MasterO'Keefe

class was given over to looking through the coloured illustrated maps and the luxury bindings of the Deluxe product of the Readers

Digest. I still never mastered Geography. Brother Perkins taught us history and science. The school had a well equipped laboratory with lots of chemicals, glass jars and pipettes etc. and so it captured my imagination. My favourite substance was mercury which had properties that amazed me. Perkins also was in charge of sports. He was quick to use the leather on any boy who didn't return for sports on Wednesday afternoon. On one occasion I took the Wednesday afternoon off to go to see the A Hard day's Night in the Star Cinema. Being a big Beatles fan I thought it was well worth the few licks of the leather I got the following afternoon. Science and English were the only subjects that I got Honours in in my Intermediate Certificate. However was nothing intermediate about my certificate, it was the last certificate I got and I left Drimnagh Castle in 1964.

The moat around Drimnagh Castle

Teresa

Auntie Teresa arrived in my life in September 1953. I remember Moira and myself sliding on the lino in the hall the day she arrived. Six months after my mum's death she had come to us as a live-in housekeeper and we were told to refer to her as auntie Teresa. She had four brothers and five sisters all from a farming background in Tullamore Co.Offally. Despite being from a rural background she had tremendous poise and grace. At twenty-one years of age she was fashion conscious and could choose and wear fashion with style. She was an excellent cook having been in domestic service in the Bishop' House in Mullingar and she often boasted of winning "a bible prize" which I understand was for winning a competition on knowing passages from the Bible. Her favourite poem was Mise Raftry an File, She loved playing cards and had a thousand wise sayings many of which were in fact country witticisms. EG *"You talk like the halfpenny book"* meaning your facts are all wrong because the Halfpenny Book was cheap on account of it's facts being all wrong. The most significant change in our lives after

Teresa's arrival was our access to the country. Both my mum Cissy and my dad were entirely city folk. They had no attachment with the country having hardly ever stirred outside Dublin. Within weeks of her arrival Teresa had myself, my dad and Moira visiting her father's farm in Ballydaly just outside Tullamore. They had cows, pigs, chickens, geese, dogs and cats, like I mean, lots of them. As far as I was concerned the donkey was the most charming animal. I could sit on his back or ride behind him in a small cart. He helped in bringing water up from the well which was about a quarter of a mile from the thatched cottage in which granny and grand-dad Leavey lived. Neddy also assisted in bringing back turf from the bog. Days on the bog were idyllic with the beautiful smells of the peat and the covering furze and delirious packed lunches accompanied by lashings of butter-milk. Behind the thatched cottage was a cow parlor where the cows were milked and housed in the winter. Next door to that was the hen-house where the fresh eggs could be found every morning. Also in this building was a mangle which was used to pulp turnips and parsnips for cattle feed. As children we most enjoyed feeding the chickens and geese. We also loved watching the calf's being fed buckets milk .in a shed in the farm yard. There was a large barn across the yard from the cottage where a year's supply of turf was banked up as high as fifteen feet high. There was no electricity in the cottage and every evening the Tilly lamps were lit. The large open fire was the centre of the household and all the cooking was done either on the hob or in bakers which were hung from iron bars over the fire. Bread and apple tarts were baked every day using these methods. Also taking pride of place in the kitchen was the dresser. The coloured plates and mugs on this dresser were displayed in such a way as to light up and brighten the kitchen both in the daytime and in the light of the Tilly lamps. Meanwhile back on Bunting Road I had just started school. Apart from ensuring that I got to school in Crumlin (a two mile walk) every day, Teresa had my three year old sister and one year old brother to look after. Over the following years Teresa took great pride in dressing us up for every special occasion. She organised my fifth birthday party which had an added poignancy as it occurred only six months after my mum's death. She did this with great verve and employed one of her greatest attributes which was the ease with she made friends with all the neighbours on Bunting Road. She was only in situ for a matter of months but she got a large number of children to attend my birthday party. Likewise I was dressed very smartly for my first communion in 1955 with my communion medal and pocket handkerchief. As time went by both Moira and Brian started school

and things went along very smoothly. Then in 1958 something unusual and unexpected suddenly happened. Auntie Teresa became mammy when she and my dad got married. They got married in the newly built Walkinstown Church. The wedding reception was held in 112 Bunting road with the neighbours providing the wedding breakfast and the three tier wedding cake. Only half of Teresa's family attended her wedding because her brother William got married on the same day in London and the family was shared out half and half to attend both weddings. Teresa then got busy and produced a further six sons and three daughters for my father who was extremely proud of his large family . Rearing twelve children was a heroic achievement for auntie Teresa. The new brothers and sisters were as follows : Oliver, Aine, Liam, Aileen, Colm, Kevin, Rory, Theresa and Ciaran. Teresa lived to be seventy four years old. She had a tough and arduous life struggling with finances and not always getting along with my dad. She dressed all twelve of us smartly for communions and confirmations, saw many of us off to the Gaeltacht with money in our pockets, did us proud at Christmas and Easter and her favorite time Halloween. My Dad taught her to drive in the 1950s and she spent half of her life behind the wheel.
She visited everybody everywhere and was always ready to jump in the car and bring somebody somewhere they would otherwise

unable to go. She was a very safe driver but shortly before she died she crashed into telephone pole. Within days she had the car repaired and the family knew nothing about it. A couple of weeks later she began having dizzy spells. My sister Aileen brought her St. James's

Hospital where they thought she was de-hydrated. After a week of tests they discovered she had advanced brain cancer. She died five days later. She had clearly been driving around with brain cancer for many months before her death. I spent two weeks tending to her in the hospital. My sister Aileen and my wife and daughter Ferga also took in turns to spend time with her. Ferga did the night shifts from midnight to 8am when I took over and fed her breakfast. She spoke to my brother Brian who was in Santa Fe New Mexico on the phone. My brothers Colm and Ciaran rushed from Sidney to be by her side before she died. My sister Aine who is a senior nurse flew over twice to be with her from Kent. Kevin Rory and Oliver came from London and Theresa came from Coventry and thankfully got to her in time to say their last farewell to a very unique and very spectacular woman. I am super proud of my seven brothers and four sisters. Brian and

From left: Theresa, Oliver, Moira, Ciaran, Colm, Liam, Brian, Aileen, Rory, Aine, Kevin and Michael

Oliver both worked in the printing for a period before Oliver went off to drive a bus in London for thirty years, Brian now drives a bus in Santa Fe, New Mexico, Aileen has her career in the passport office, Liam is a senior manager in Microsoft, Ciaran is an accountant in Sidney, Theresa was a restaurant manager in Coventry, Moira had her Seven Eleven in Cavan, Kevin is a "chippie" in London, Rory manages a bathroom emporium in London and Aine is a specialist in midwifery who travels the world advising developing countries on the safest methods of child birth delivery.

The Apollo Gang

The Apollo gang were a group friends that hung around the Apollo Cinema and the Snack Bar beside the cinema in and around 1965. Our interests mainly surrounded music, dancing and fashion. The group included Frank Murray, Paul Scully, Laurance Corrigan, Tommy Hegerty, Frannie Lennon, Evelyn Buckley, Mary and Angela Courtney, Phyliss Hall, Declan Collinge. John Doyle, Des and Pete McMahon and Shay McCarthy. On occasions we were joined by Philip Lynott. Our activities centered around the Snack Bar beside the Apollo cinema. This was a converted garage barely big enough to hold a single car such as you would have beside any average house. It was owned by Leggio's chipper next door and it had a hatch which allowed chips to be handed through to the snack bar. It's difficult to describe how little money any of us had, most were still in secondary school and relied on pocket money from parents.

Adults did not frequent this tiny little cafe and so the menu contained one item "a plate of chips." The only drinks on sale were different flavours of Fanta. I'm not sure if Coca Cola had even reached Ireland in 1965. So it was that we shared plates of chips, bottles of Fanta and Club Milks. We discussed the Beatles, the Rolling Stones, the Animals, and Them. The Belfast band Them were huge at the time with songs like Here Comes The Night and Gloria. Their lead singer was Van Morrison but we didn't consider him important, we loved the songs but with John, Paul, George,

Ringo and Mick Jagger at the forefront of our minds Van Morrison hardly registered. Fashion was very important in our world then, not just among the girls but among the guys also. Mary Quant was setting the style for girls with black and white geometric designs and very short skirts. Twiggy was the most popular model and the fashions changed every week. This was an age where you had to keep up with fashion. Unlike today when everything goes and multiple styles co-exist, you had to have the latest. The lads too had to keep up with the fashion. Cuff links were all the rage. You had to show two inches of a white cuff so you could show off your new cuff links. Skinny ties and granny print shirts and granny print ties were obligatory. "Even Steven" was a shop in Capel Street which sold all the latest "gear" which was a word that came into our vocabulary about that time. The Reefer jacket became ubiquitous at that time. Philip Lynott had a great sense of style and he influenced us to shop in the Iveagh Market were clothes from a different era were on sale at low cost. Then we progressed to the army surplus stores where navy uniforms and great coats with epaulettes gave a great sense of style and gravitas to one's rig out. Of course the

Apollo cinema was also central to our lives. It was the most important institution in Walkinstown apart from the church. We had been going to the pictures in the Apollo from the time we were children. But now it took on a whole new function. While it is true that we were packed in two to a seat as children on Saturday afternoons it is important to say how beautiful the Apollo Cinema in Walkinstown was. When we went there as teenagers it was a wonderful experience. We went there in groups with several couples trying out their first dates under the watchful eyes of their pals and after a film show everyone would know which guy put his arm around which girl and who got a kiss. Before the film started and we were often in half an hour early and the latest pop songs would be played on the Cinema sound system which was very moving in the the plush atmosphere of the cinema. I particularly remember the Beatles song "Things We Said Today" being played and this summed up our experience of the magical teenage years at that time. And then on Friday nights many bands (pop groups) played to packed houses after the last film show. Among them the Black Eagles and Ditch Cassidy and the News. All this has to be taken in the context that luxuries in the 1960s were very few. Few had central heating in their homes and peoples homes were often very cold. As

Findlaters said in an article published about their branch in Walkinstown, people in the area were poor, sweets and lemonade biscuits and cakes were rare and expensive and obesity hadn't been invented. So it was that the Apollo was a haven from austerity even though that term hadn't been coined. The Apollo was one of the only facilities in Walkinstown which gave the place character. It was so sad that this beautiful facility was pulled down to make space for half a dozen houses. Of course the Apollo gang had other places to congregate chief among them was the Moeran Hall. This was where boy really met girl. It was in the phrase of the time "a record hop." The girls lined up on one side of the hall and the boys on the other. Dances were either slow or fast and divided in to gents choice, ladies choice and sometimes mixed choice. You marched across the floor and asked a girl to dance. Refusals were few but a girl could let you know very quickly that she didn't want you to ask her up again. These were much more innocent times and a walk home and a kiss at the gate was all that anyone could aspire to. As I was particularly small I normally had to sit out a lady's choice. One brave and delightful young lady, Joan Sherry asked me up for a slow dance. This was like winning the Lotto for me and naturally I asked her out

on a date. We went to Apollo where the film Zulu was playing. She later told me that she was embarrassed by the nudity of the Zulu women in the film. Though we went our separate ways we are still in touch and she still retains all the charms that she had in 1965. Another young lady I danced with occasionally at the same venue was Lilly Hennessy. Always with a smiley face she was a very fun loving girl. Both of these girls are now grannies with wonderful families having lived wonderful lives. Such were the encounters and outcrops of dancing in the Moeran Hall in the 1960s and such was the tale of the Apollo gang. In 1965 I made a cine film entitled The Apollo Gang and it can be viewed on Youtube.

Cannon Hickey

Cannon Hickey was our parish priest when Walkinstown was still part of the Crumlin Parish. When I started school in 1953 most of the children from Walkinstown went to school in Crumlin and I went to the National School on St.. Agnes Road. The school was totally over-subscribed and my dad had trouble getting me into school. So my Dad brought me to the Presbytery for an interview with Canon Hickey. My Dad said he was thinking of sending me to the local Protestant school where there were lots vacancies. The canon wasn't amused but he relented and agreed to instruct the school principle to take me in. When I made my first communion in 1955 Cannon Hickey gave every child in the school a bag of sweets and some fruit. I think this was because the children in the Nuns school on Armagh Road all got a free breakfast of eggs and rashers on their communion day. . Cannon Hickey always carried a black thorn stick and used it regularly on the boys who stood up on the railings outside St. Agnes Church after Mass on Sundays. Fr. Burke who was later Parish priest in Walkinstown used to say the 10 o'clock Mass in st. Agnes Church and I often hear him tell mothers to take their crying children out of the church. I also heard him giving out to the alter boys when they got things wrong. We used to enter the Church from the Dowland Road gate. Every year the Canon organised a carnival to raise money for Church funds in the waste ground behind St. Agnes's Chruch .You could enter the carnival grounds from the gate on Dowland Road in Walkinstown. It was one of the most entertaining events to occur every year in the area. Apart from the fun rides for the children, teenage boys and girls had an opportunity to meet and mix, share ice creams buy each other lemonade. A big feature at the carnival was the Wheel of Fortune. This involved

buying tickets and standing around until sufficient tickets had been sold. Then the guy would spin the wheel and when it stopped he would call out the winning number. If you won you could then choose any of item on show. When you claimed your prize the guy would say " winner alright and off we go again." I once won a gold fish and my mum won a set of cups and saucers. The carnival was canceled on the news of the death of Pope Pius XII in 1958.

The Boxing Club

Believe it or not myself and my brother Brian went to both boxing and Irish dance classes in the same room (a kind of shed) beside the National School on St. Agnes' Road. This was before there were any facilities in Walkinstown. While the boxing was restricted to the boys, the Irish dancing was mixed with boys and girls in the same class. I lost interest in the boxing after getting a broken and bloody nose and I lost interest in the Irish dancing classes because only the girls had fancy costumes.

Tallaght Village

The Cuckoo's Nest

Picking blackberries on the Greenhill's Road

The Road to Tallaght

Hundreds of people from the newly built Walkinstown in the 1950s and early 1960s used take a walk up the Greenhills road every Sunday afternoon in the summer and many stopped to pick black berries. while others carried on past the two dumps on either sides of the road and past the big old house on the right hand side at the brow of the hill where large numbers of rabbits could been seen roaming around in the fields. Then on down the hill towards the Cuckoo's nest (there was no bridge over the M50 then) and again up the next hill and the last little crooked road that led to the village of Tallaght. I often took this walk early on Sunday mornings (when my Dad thought I was off to Mass) and carried on down Firhouse road turning in beside the graveyard on the Wellington Road and all the way down to the Submarine Bar. Then back up Cromwellsfort Road and down John McCormick's Avenue and back to Bunting Road. It was at it's most beautiful in the Winter when the snow lay on the Greenhills Road without a single footprint on it. The Greenhills road is an ancient road carved out by a glacier more than ten thousand years ago during the last ice age. This link between the city of Dublin and Tallaght can be seen on maps going back hundreds of years. All along this route high over the city were quarries where sand was dug out for construction over hundreds of years leaving a scarred landscape which when the grass grew over it, it became the Greenhills.

The Quarry

Then there was the quarry behind the Submarine Bar. I often passed it on my walks down Wellington Lane but I never swam in it. However some of my friends were not so cowardly and they often jumped in. Of course there was more than one quarry in the locality and many children were drowned in these quarries. I used to walk down Wellington lane to the Submarine Bar and back up Cromwellsfort Road again on Sunday mornings on my way back from Tallaght village to view the beauty and to avoid going to Mass Disused for nearly fifty years the quarry varied in depth from twenty to thirty feet with pockets as deep as fifty feet. Over the years it had taken a number of children's lives, nobody could be sure how many but in 1947 local people had a fence erected around it for safety reasons. However the children continued to climb over it in summer to swim and in winter to skate on the ice. The quarry had a mesmerising beauty in both summer and winter and as such it had a fatal attraction. When we were teenagers we often went down to the quarry just to throw stones into it and then call into Borza's chipper on the Cromwellsfort road on the way back. This quarry was subsequently filled in and built over and it is now part of the greater Walkinstown area.

Ballymount Lane

I always loved the shops and cottages on Ballymount Lane as we called it. Some of the residents of the cottages kept pigs, chickens and ponies. We loved going up to see them. Also the first shop on the row was the Monument Creamery where we could buy butter by the ounce. The butter was cut out of a large block of butter with a pair wooden butter pats and served in a packet of grease-proof paper.

It was often along Ballymount lane that we ventured out on hikes with sandwiches packed in our little haversacks. Along the road we passed the tinkers in their tents until we came to the ruins of Ballymont castle in the middle of a wild set of green hills. Sadly it's an industrial estate now and the lovely flora and fauna have vanished

Na Fianna Eireann

Feargal O'Hanlon died on 1st January 1957 He was killed along with Seán South while taking part in an attack on the Royal Ulster Constabulary (R.U.C.) barracks in Brookeborough, County Fermanagh, during the 1950s Border Campaign. Several other IRA members were wounded in the botched attack. The IRA fled the scene in a dumper truck. They abandoned it near the border. They left South and O'Hanlon, both of them unconscious, in a cow byre, and crossed into the Republic of Ireland on foot seeking for help for their comrades. These events and personalities are sympathetically recalled in Dominic Behan's ballad..

The Patriot Game.

Come all you young rebels and list while I sing
For love of ones land is a terrible thing
It banishes fear with the speed of a flame
And makes us all part of the patriot game
My name is O'Hanlon, I'm just gone sixteen
My home is in Monaghan there I was weaned
I learned all my life cruel England to blame
And so I'm part of the patriot game

I joined Na Fianna Eireann in September 1957 aged 9 years old and not long after the death of Fergal O'Hanlon. Naturally as a 9 year old I had no idea of the political significance of Na Fianna Eireann.

This boy scout organisation was banned and illegal but for me it was a great adventure. At our weekly scout meetings which took place in Ard Scoil Eanna on the Crumlin road we were taught all the usual things that boy scouts the world over learn and practice. Knots, Semifore, Morse code camping craft and first aid. We also learned the history of Na Fianna from the time of Fionn MacCool up until it's re-invention by Bulmer Hobson, Countess Markievicz, Con Colbert and Liam Mellows. We were taught the Fianna Motto and the Fianna Code of Honour and we learned about the Fianna flag and The Easter Rising of 1916. However what captured my mind most was the prospect of going off into forests and the countryside camping and hiking, climbing trees and making tools for use in the wild. Most Sunday mornings in the summer we all joined up to get the bus from College Green to Pine Forest Enniskerry or the Scalp. We brought potatoes, sausages and tiny tins of beans. Everywhere we went we lit camp fires and skewered our sausages and held them over the fire. The beans and the potatoes were wrapped in wet grass and buried under the fire and then dug up again cooked and ready eat. Elaborate hanging devices were made from gathered wood and sticks for suspending billy cans and pots over the fire to make tea or soup. One of the most treasured items was a volcano kettle which allowed one to put fire inside the kettle to very rapidly boil a cup of water. This was particularly useful in stormy or wet weather. Lighting fires in windy or wet conditions was a skill that every scout had to learn the hard way. Tools employed in wood craft included jack-knives and axes and all young scouts looked forward to getting their own axe or jack-knife. The jack-knife was worn in a sheath attached to the scout's belt and became part of the scout uniform alongside the scout lanyard and the scout whistle. Senior Fianna officers also wore Sam Brown belts which gave their uniforms a military look. They also wore slouch hats which were redolent of the Volunteers who fought in the 1916 Rebellion. As Fianna boys we had other duies. We formed up the colour parties for the annual commemorations of the 1916 Rebellion every Easter. We marched at the head of the parades from the GPO to Glassnevin Cemetery or sometime from Berkley Road Church to Glasnevin were flags were lowered, bugles blown and wreaths laid. Then there where long and boring speeches all while I was thinking about my Easter eggs. In 1962 I was part of the colour party which marched to Deans Grange Cemetery where it was announced that the 1950s IRA Border Campaign was to be called off. In 1959 which was the 100th Anniversary of the founding of the Fianna a huge gathering or jamboree of Fianna boys from all over Ireland was held at Poulaphouca in County Wicklow. It was intended to be a three day camp and myself and my brother Brian were delighted to be allowed attend. A lorry picked us all up and drove to the camp site. Everything was ship shape just as all of us boy scouts were trained to do. Tents up, guy ropes secured, seats and tables made from wood and branches ,fires lit, flags flown and we all drilled and saluted our officers, it was a great feeling of comradeship and achievement. It was a beautiful sunny day and some of the officers went swimming

in the Poulaphouca lakes. Eventually we had our meal, it got dark and we retired to our tents. About eleven o'clock that night an electrical storm broke out with sheath lightening brightening up the whole sky so that it was as bright as daylight, so much so that the officers were able to take photographs without flash. Then the rain came and we were all caught out in the open and everyone got soaked to the skin. As no one had dry clothes it was decided that all the younger scouts would have to be brought home the following day. As it turned out hundreds of car windscreens had been smashed by the lightening on that night. I had saved up my pocket money for months to go on this camp and I felt cheated that I only got one day instead of three. However I enjoyed many camps and hikes with the Fianna and enjoyed many sing-songs by campfires at night over the following four years. I left the Fianna in 1963 when I got a summer job in The Royal Hibernian Hotel.

The Royal Hibernian Hotel

Dublin in 1963 was a very small place. There were few people and very few job opportunities. So at fifteen years old I set out to find a summer job. I tried a few hotels without success until I climbed the granite steps of the Royal Hibernian Hotel. I spoke to the Head Hall porter Tom Curran and asked him for a start. Being particularly small he didn't consider having me as a porter carrying large suit cases from the hall to the guests rooms. He offered me a job as a pageboy. This suited me, literally, down to the ground. What was most attractive to me was the uniform which included a pair of long trousers and believe it or not. I had never owned or worn a pair of long trousers up to that point. My induction to the job included getting a fitting for my first pair of long trousers. Once in uniform I was given a list of my duties as a page boy. This included carrying letters on a silver salver to the guests in their rooms, calling guests to take telephone calls at the reception desk, manning the hotel exchange and putting through calls through to guests in their rooms and driving the elevator which was manually operated and had a cage like sliding door. Driving the elevator was a lot of fun because it climbed very slowly and descended very fast often over-shooting the floor at which the guests wished to exit. Thus it was common enough for very wealthy high ranking officials and international

celebrities to find themselves in the grubby basement of what was an otherwise super high class luxury hotel. However, driving the lift was the best part of the job because invariably guests who spent more than a couple of days in the hotel always struck up a friendship with the lift boy and multiple tips followed. In 1963 the actor Christopher Plummer was resident in the hotel and I saw him nearly every day for a month. He was a generous tipper. Within the Hibernian Hotel there were two internationally renowned venues where celebrities, actors and politicians used to congregate. They were The Buttery bar and The Lafayette restaurant. One of my jobs was to hover the very plush red carpet in the restaurant. This enabled me to pinch a hand full of chocolate gold grain biscuits which were always on hand and on display. Another job I had was to clean the brasses. The hotel had too magnificent brass rails on either side of the steps at the front entrance to the building. These gleamed in the sunlight adding an air of magnificence to the hotel as it faced down Molesworth street mirroring the entrance to Dail Eireann. During my time at the Hibernian Hotel in 1963, President Kennedy visited Dublin and I was able to go to Dublin Castle during my lunch hour and see him leaving the castle in an open top car waving to the crowd and sporting an incredible tan clearly visible from twenty yards away. This had an added significance because having completed my intermediate certificate in 1964 I returned to the hotel for another summer and accumulated numerous half dollar tips from

American tourists anxious to display the specially minted half dollar coins in memory of the recently slain John. F. Kennedy. The owner of the hotel was a Mr. Besson who resided at the hotel and the General manager was a Mr. Manasero who particularly impressed me with his style and business like attitude. As I often stood beside him in his office holding my silver salver with a letter for him he rattled off orders on the telephone without a hmm or a haw and then quickly dialed another number and spoke just as urgently to the next person at the other end. Fifty years later I am still convinced that he was doing this simply to educate me in how to do business. Having been brought over from France by Mr. Besson to run the hotel he demonstrated quality in his every action. I left the hotel in September 1964 to take my up apprenticeship in the printing.

Philip Lynott

I first got to know Philip Lynott in 1965 when the Black Eagles played in the Moeran Hall in Walkinstown. The Black Eagles were the most popular bands to play in the hall which was a community hall built by the Walkinstown Residents Association under the leadership Joe Connolly who also founded the Community Games association. There were very few halls of this type in Dublin at that time. Other bands that played in this hall included Some People, The News, The Dead Centre and the Chessmen. I brought a camera to the dance which was a very unusual thing to do at that time. It was a Rolyflex camera belonging to my father who was big into photography. I took some photos of the band on stage and Philip came down from the stage at the interval and asked me if he could have copies of the photographs. He invited myself and Frank Murray to his house in Leiglin Road and I brought the photographs and we became firm friends. Frank became a roadie with the band and with subsequent bands ie .Skid Row and Thin Lizzy. Soon after I brought the photos to Philip's house, myself and Frank began to attend band practice in Ard Scoil Eanna on the Crumlin road where I took more photos of the band outside the walls of the practice hall. I then told Philip that I intended to make a film of the band and he asked me if it would be in colour or black and white. I said colour thinking he be impressed but he said he came out better in black and white. This was an early example of Philip's sense of humour. He also said about that time how much enjoyed it when young children pointed to him on the bus and said "mammy, mammy there's a black man." There weren't many coloured people in Dublin at that time. Philip is on record on the Late Late Show as saying he never encountered any racism when he was young. Asked if he was given a hard time because of his colour he said "it was no worse than having

Philip Lynott and the Black Eagles outside the Moeran Hall in 1965
Copyright Michael O'Flanagan

cauliflower ears." Sometime in mid-summer 1965 we made the film using a Bollex D-8L three turret 8mm ciné camera. My uncle Sean had come home from South Africa the previous year and brought his ciné camera and projector with him. Previous to this we had never heard of films being shown in a normal house. It turned out that television was banned in South Africa and most white families there had their own home cinemas. Of course my father who was obsessed with photography was hugely impressed and set out to get a camera and projector as soon as possible. As I was my father's favourite it took me no time at all to persuade him to loan me the camera and I very soon learned how to load it and shoot film. The Camera was hand wound but a single winding of the camera would be sufficient to keep the camera running to the twenty-five feet of film on a normal reel. Although the Camera was an 8mm camera, the film used as 16mm which was run once, turned over and then run backwards through the camera giving a total of fifty feet per spool. The Film was then split and spliced at processing. The camera had three turrets to allow various focal lengths of shot. The standard lens allowed filming from 10 to 25 feet, the Telephoto lens allowed filming from 25 feet to infinity and the wide angle lens was for taking shots of large groups. Filming had to be stopped in order to change lens so that if a long shot on telephoto was being filmed and the subject came towards the camera their heads were cut off because the lens had not been changed to the standard or wide angle

This is a photograph of me taking a photo of Philip taking this photo of me

lens. Philip appointed himself director of the film. It was less than a year since the Film "A Hard Day's Night" by the Beatles had been screened in the local Star Cinema. Philip wanted to recreate many of the antics and tricks that had been employed in the Beatles film. So it was that one of the first scenes is a fight scene outside the old police station in Crumlin village. This was followed by shots of the various members of the band marching along outside the old cottages in the village. The next scene is all of the band charging towards the camera in Mooney's field. Then they are seated for a few moments until Philip throws up his yellow hankerchief as a signal to start another fight. Then a stone is dropped into a puddle to mark an interval and a change of scene. The party then moves up to the Walkinstown library where once again the lads walk towards the camera. The next scene is the band outside the Moeran Hall banging the door trying to get in. This was Philip's idea and when the film was shown some weeks later as the Black eagles were playing in the same hall the crowd went wild. Seeing your local area on film or TV was very rare in those days. Myself and Frank Murray lived in Walkinstown and Philip often came up to Walkinstown to hang out with us at The Snack Bar beside The Apollo Cinema. Philip attended my 18th Birthday party in my home on Bunting Road in 1966. He bought me a pocket transistor radio as a birthday present and I had kept a half bottle of Vodka specially for him at the party. However, Philip wasn't a big drinker in those early days. Joe Smith was the manager of The Black Eagles. Two of his sons Danny and Frankie were also members of the band. Frankie left the band, some said that he had run away with his girlfriend. Each member of the band was paid 10 shillings per gig and Joe Smith paid for a holiday for them in Butlins once a year. However he totally controlled the band. He owned all the equipment , amplifiers, microphones, guitars, drums etc including the bandwaggon. The only thing that Philip owned was the Binson Echo which he was buying on the hire purchase. Sometime in 1966 The Black Eagles broke up. During this period Philip's favourite hang out was the Go Go Club just off O'Connell Street in Dublin. Philip was friendly with Stevie Bolger who was the most popular DJ at the club and Philip never missed seeing The Grannies Intentions who played there nearly every week. I often gave Philip a lift home from The Go Go on my Honda motor bike. Some times he took taxis. Most of the Taxi-drivers had no idea who Philip was. He used to let on he was a Nigerian student at TCD and would talk in pigeon English to the taxi-drivers. On one occasion when he arrived home in Crumlin the taxi-driver told him that the fare would be 10 Shillings. Suddenly Philip reverted back to his broad Dublin accent and said it was not 10 Shillings but only 7 Shillings and 6 pence as it had been every other night. However the taxi-driver still insisted that it was 10 Shillings. Philip said " you better take me around to the cop shop then and we'll see what it is."

The taxi-driver then relented and slid a half-crown across the seat to Philip, thinking that Philip would say "it's ok, you can keep it." But Philip took the money, pocketed it, got out of the taxi and walked away. Then the taxi-driver jumped out of the taxi and shouted after Philip "I'm glad they shot Martin Luther King" which they had that very day. The following year Brush Shiels invited Philip to join Skid Row. The new band consisted of Brush Shiels, Noel Bridgeman, Bernard Cheevers and Philip. Noel had come up with the name in a Whimpey Bar in Dorset Street. They practiced in Mrs Quigley's house in Synnot Place off Dorset Street. Philip introduced me to Brush and told him that I would be making films and taking photos of the band. I attended their first gig in UCD in Earlsfort Terrace where Brush ripped Philip's shirt off him in the middle of a number. Both Philip and Brush were anxious to use my film projector as part of their act as they knew that The Velvet Underground were doing something similar in New York. I showed black and white films of President Kennedy being shot as a backdrop to the band playing on stage. On one occasion I showed a film of the Pope visiting the Holy Land. Philip was singing a song called "Sky Pilot" by Eric Burdon of the Animals. The event took place in the CYMS in Fairview which was a kind of Parish Hall. One of the local officials took offence and the incident was reported on the front page of the Evening Herald as "group perform blasphemous song at local dance." Philip was delighted with the publicity but Brush's mother was horrified when she heard about it. We then decided to make films in the Beat Clubs. This was no easy matter as the lighting was very poor and all of the equipment I had was amateur equipment. I had to bring in a hand held flood light and this was very disruptive of the dancing of the young people who paid the bills. Nonetheless we managed to capture some of the atmosphere of that time even though that was not the reason we were doing it at the time. Philip and Brush were more interested in creating a "vibe" at the gigs. On one occasion we decided to do some filming in the Dublin Mountains. None of us had a car so we all climbed onto a Dublin bus. As the bus reached the rural area we noticed that there was a crane on the back of a truck in front of the bus. The bus was gradually getting closer and closer to the truck. Suddenly the truck in front stopped but the bus kept going. The crane came in through the front window of the upper floor of the double-decker bus. Myself and Philip were in the front seat. Although we both ducked down we both got a shower of glass into our hair. After a few minutes another bus came along and we continued on up the mountain to complete our filming. I got a very memorable shot of Gary Moore smoking in the open air. The rest of the film is of the lads picking blackberries from the ditches along the mountain road. I used to

SKID ROW

attend band practice in a garage behind the Black Church in Phibsboro. On a number of occasions band practice was canceled because Brush's mother was very ill. Then myself and Philip would head off on my Honda to the Grafton Cinema to watch cartoons. Philip always loved comics and cartoons. That's how he later came up with the name Thin Lizzy for his new band. The line-up of Skid Row group changed several times. Bernard Cheevers, the first guitarist with the group was an electrician with a well paid job in Guinness. He saw the band as an extra source of income and although a highly accomplished musician he was reluctant to go fully professional. He was replaced by Gary Moore who was from Belfast and who came to Dublin to stand in for Dave Lewis of the Method who had been injured in a car accident. Gary Moore was

primarily a blues guitarist doing a lot of Cream, Fleetwood Mac and Traffic numbers. Bernard Cheevers had a wide knowledge of music and could play Hendrix numbers with his teeth. It is also worth pointing out that Philip had a very wide repertoire and when he was with the Black Eagles he sang songs by The Four Tops (If I Were A Carpenter) Dusty Springfield (I think I'm Going Back) and the Who (My Generation and Boris is a Spider) I loaned him an LP of Etta James so he could learn some of her songs. While with Skid Row Philip favoured progressive rock and psychedelic music . He did a great performance of "I am The Walrus" by the Beatles. Noel Bridgeman was an important member of the band too both as a drummer and as a singer. He did the harmonies and sang a couple of songs by The Byrds. Skid Row were invited to guest on an RTE Television Show called "Like Now." The Show was recorded in the Top Hat Ballroom in Dun Laoghaire. When the Show was broadcast Noel resigned from the band because Philip had failed to sing in key. Robbie Brennan then joined as drummer and some thought that this was the best line-up of the band with with Philip, Gary, Brush and Robbie. However this band did not last very long and Brush sacked Philip from the band but taught him how to play the bass guitar. Robbie also left the band at this time and Noel Bridgeman came back making Skid Row a three piece band aka Cream. I continued to work with Skid Row until they left for England. Philip invited me over to his apartment in Clontarf to meet his new band Thin Lizzy and I took some photographs of the band in the house and on the seafront. My friend Terry O'Neill was the band's first Manager. Fran Quigley was the band's first road manager and my other friend Frank Murray became the chief roadie for Thin Lizzy. I took photo's of the

SKID ROW
Up in the Dublin Mountains 1968

band in the National Stadium but I never made any movie films of Thin Lizzy. I remained friends with Philip over the years, I met him a number of times by appointment and gave him old photos, videos and slides. He always invited me back-stage whenever he had a concert in Dublin and he invited me to his birthday party in Celbridge House where I showed the old films from the early days. My silent movies of the Black Eagles and Skid Row have been used in documentaries on RTE, BBC4 and BBC Northern Ireland. Philip's early attempts at song writing were very poor, indeed his first song which was the B side of the first Skid Row single was written about me under the title of "Photograph Man." Philip's skill with lyrics improved through his interest in poetry and he published three books of poetry. I was unaware of Philip's keen interest in poetry at the time (myself and Brush published a book of poetry together in 1969) and this becomes ironic as I have edited a poetry magazine for the last 20 years. Since then I have published three collections of

my own poetry entitled, Immutability, Peep Into The Abyss and Positive fruit. My own opinion of Philip Lynott having been close to him in the early days was he had a great sense of style, was an excellent showman and had powerful presence on stage. Next to Queen, Thin Lizzy was the best live band in the world because Philip had such an excellent rapport with the audience. However, I am always conscious that Thin Lizzy was a band and not just a singer. While Philip always enjoyed the limelight the pressures of constant touring affected him deeply. I am sure that he was happiest in the early days of The Black Eagles.

Brush Shiels

Philip introduced me to Brush Shiels in Mrs Quigley's house in Synnott Place of Dorset Street shortly after the Black Eagles broke up. Pat Quigley was the lead singer in The Movement and his brother Fran Quigley was a specialist in sound equipment. At that time Brush had a higher profile than Philip as he had been a big success in playing in The Uptown Band with Peter Adler and Mojo. Brush had formed a new band called Skid Row and he invited Philip to be the lead singer. Philip introduced me to Brush saying that I would be making films and taking photos of the band. It's difficult to stress how little money all of these guys had and anyone who would

take photos and be making films of the band free of charge was welcomed with open arms. Few people had good camera's or movie camera's. Everyone was in awe of Brush because he had the gift of the gab and had huge powers of persuasion. This enabled him to negotiate great deals and multiple gigs on behalf of the band. For example he got the band gigs in Barry's Hotel and the Irene Ballroom where pop groups and rock bands were normally excluded because they didn't feature brass instruments. Brass was essential for Show Bands and they normally controlled the Ballrooms where the largest crowds gathered. The larger the crowds the bigger the fee. From the outset I got along great with Brush and his girl friend Margaret Reilly. She lived next door to Noel Bridgeman who was

the drummer in Skid Row and it was Noel who came up the name for the band in the Whimpy Bar in Dorset Street. I took photographs and made a movies of Brush's wedding. When they lived in a flat on the South Circular road I bought them a pair of goldfish which they had for several years. I traveled the country with Skid Row and all along the way I listened to Brush who was a font of knowledge about the music business in Ireland. Brush was interviewed on RTE about the music scene Dublin. In the 1960s the interview was considered shocking because he said that "all dance music is sexually inspired." Brush had learned his craft as a bass player with Rose Tynan's show band but with Skid Row he was determined to write and play original rock music in style of Cream, Deep Purple Steppenwolf. Gary Moore wanted to play Blues and Philip was into progressive rock and the Velvet Underground. After Philip left Skid Row I continued to work with Brush and I made several more films of the band both indoor and outdoor. It was always difficult to film in the dark atmosphere of the Dublin Beat Clubs. When the band moved to London Brush invited me to go with the band. I spent several weeks with them and made a film of the band traveling on the Tube. London wasn't very much to my liking and I returned to Dublin and my new girlfriend Helena who was a member of the Skid Row fan club shortly before they went to London. Skid Row spent several years in England and toured the world including the USA.

Paul, Fredie, Moe and Brush Shiels at the National Stadium 1970

They came back to Ireland regularly and played in the National Stadium. In 1970 the band played a concert in the Countdown Club. I took a series of colour photos of the band and these have been of great value in many TV programs and in several books published on the era of the early pop and rock bands in Ireland. Myself and my

wife Helena have remained close friends with Brush and his wife Margaret for nearly fifty years and he has always been there for me and supported me and all my projects over the years.

Gary Moore

Frank Murray found Gary Moore playing in the e Go Go Club. Gary had come down from Belfast to stand in for Dave Lewis, the lead guitarist in the Method. Dave had been injured in a car crash and Gary fitted in grand because they played all Cream numbers and he could play the Blues to perfection. The drummer has a twenty-six inch cymbal so he could play Tales of Brave Ulysses. Everyone was knocked out with Gary's guitar skills and Brush recruited him immediately saying goodbye to Bernard Cheevers. Gary was obsessed with the guitar and paid scant attention to his personal appearance or indeed anything else. Brush's wife Margaret bought him clothes in the second hand markets and suddenly he looked very hip with corduroy trousers, kaftans and wide collared shirts. He let

his hair grow wild and just pushed it up onto the top of his head. He smoked a lot even when playing the guitar on stage. I acted as his guide and escorted him to the bar or sometimes the jacks. He stayed in my flat in Manor street on a number of occasions. Apart from the members of the band Gary's closest friend was Ivan Pawle who was a member of the band Strangely Strange. Gary often stayed in their house in Sandymount. . They used ping pong bats and jars of peas for percussion and they carried around a harmonium (or church organ) as a wind instrument. I visited their house once and saw a block of cannabis resin the size of a bar of sunlight soap on the mantle piece beside the harmonium. It was all very zaney! While everyone recognised Gary's exceptional skill as a guitarist few paid enough attention to the quality of his singing voice. He was very soft spoken but he could sing most beautifully. He never exploited this to maximum effect and even in his solo career he placed too much emphasis on his guitar work. This brought him recognition form all his great contemporaries, Green, Mayall, Gallagher and Buddy Guy but he missed out on a great opportunity to be a great singer. When Gary was with Skid Row I traveled all over Ireland with him. I

shared a bedroom with him in London when the band moved to England. He enjoyed playing the guitar morning, noon and night. I filmed him in nearly every situation. When he died I gave all my films of him to the BBC and they used it all in their documentary "Still Got The Blues." It was a great privilege to have known Gary.

DOLLARDS

I started my apprenticeship in Dollards in September 1964 having passed the printers exam. This exam was only open to printers sons and vacancies in apprenticeships were guaranteed to printers sons who passed the exam. So I got my apprenticeship as a printer to operate printing machines and actually produce the finished product. My father, grandfather and great-grandfather were all printers but they were compositors composing the type letter by letter and line by line locking them up in frames for transport to the printing machines. I on the other hand was about to start out on career of operating printing machines of all shapes and sizes antique and new. I had also passed the colour test which was essential as printers had to mix their own printing inks in hundreds of different colours. On my first day in Dollards the works manager Dessie McCormack took out a measuring tape and measured me in front of the girls in reception. This was pretty humiliating but in my case it was understandable as I was only five feet tall and some of the machines

I was about operate were very large and the work required considerable strength to lift heavy chases onto the beds of printing machines. He must have been satisfied because he gave me the go ahead to turn up the following Monday morning. I was apprenticed to a Mr. Paddy Richardson who taught me the rudiments of printing. The first printing machine I learned how to operate was a Heidleberg platen. This was a letterpress machine whereby you

inserted a chase containing a form of type cast from lead into the bed of the machine. A series of rollers then rolled over the type depositing a layer of ink and then the platen closed and the paper was pressed against the type leaving the imprint of the forme on the paper which was held in place on the platen. This machine had a rotating arm which placed each sheet of paper on the platen and then quickly removed it after the print had been made. This arm was an extremely dangerous part of the machine and could slice your face off if you didn't keep your head out of the way. The first important lesson Paddy Richardson imparted to me was how "knock up" paper. You cannot put loosely scattered paper in any printing machine. The edges of all sheets of paper going into a printing machine must be perfectly aligned To "knock up" the paper you have to gather the paper loosely in your hand allowing each sheet to slide up and down between your fingers and then bang the edges together on a flat surface so that all the edges come together and align perfectly. This can only be done correctly after much practice. Now reading about the technicalities of printing can be very boring but there was nothing boring about working in Dollards. The building itself was built in 1886 fronting onto the quays, on the site of the original Custom House by Thomas Burgh, and the design with its arched entrances and dormer windows is very reminiscent of Burgh's work. The rear of the building with its exposed basement on Essex street is much more severe. The old Custom House of 1707 was a three storey building with a mansarded roof and was used as a barracks for a time until it was demolished in the late 1880s. Burgh Quay was called after this architect. In all there were five floors in Dollards if you count the basement and it's very important to count the basement because this is actually where the printing took place. On the first floor was the dispatch and first bindery This was where books and pamphlets were bound using heavy mechanical staplers.

These were all operated by girls. They also operated the folding machines which folded very large sheets several times resulting in as many as sixteen pages from one sheet of paper. On the second floor was the upper bindery where hard back books were bound. The book binders here were all men, members of the book binders union. They served an apprenticeship of seven years to learn how to hand-sew and bind and gild books in leather. On the third floor was the caseroom where the compositors set the type by hand and locked the pages of metal type up in heavy iron chases. This was called caseroom because all the different type faces were held in cases like large sliding drawers from which each letter had to be picked out letter by letter and added to a "stick' until each sentence was composed. .Also on this floor were the monotype and linotype machines which cast type mechanically enabling setting to be done much faster but which were very restricted in the typefaces they could produce. Dollards were the first printing company to print coloured postcards, you know those ones you could buy in any town in Ireland showing views of the local town. They controlled this market for nearly half a century. However by the 1960s the John Hynde company was producing a superior postcard using better quality photographs and printing them by lithography. The majority of the machinery in Dollards was letterpress machinery and I trained as a letterpress printer. In a sense I feel proud to be connected all the way back to Gutenberg who invented letterpress printing. However this presented difficulties for me later in life when nearly all printing was done by Lithography. Because letterpress printers and lithographic were controlled by two different trade unions it was hard to change from one method to the other. Meanwhile in Dollards I met up with some lovely people. I struck up a close friendship with Tony Cullen who was a year ahead of me in apprenticeship terms. He had an electric guitar and he visited all the folk clubs. He was a Beatle fan and adopted a Paul McCartney style haircut. He introduced me to the Go Go Club, the Old Triangle Club and Slatery's of Capel Street where both pop music and folk music co-existed. The machine room manager was one Leo Kavanagh. He was a soft spoken man and he chose which 'job' to give me to print. He had an office or 'box' in the middle of the machine with large intray of 'dockets' or envelopes with instructions inside detailing the work to be done. What amazed me was that as he leafed through these dockets I could see that some of the orders had been placed more than a year previously. Just imagine having to wait a year to have your Wedding invitation printed! Such was the era that I served my time in. Another friend I made was one John Field. He had the same name as a famous Irish composer and he loved classical music. He attended the Proms in England every year.

However in the era of the Beatles and the Rolling Stones he failed to spark my interest in Mozart or Beethoven. John was a transport man, his job was to bring paper and ink to my machine. It was also his job to 'wash-up" my machine by which I mean clean away the un-used ink from the 'ducts." As a 'printer' and a "craftsman" I was not permitted to pull pallets of paper around the factory or to wash-up my own machine. Neither was he allowed to print anything. Any infringement of these distinctions could well result in a trade dispute between two unions and even a strike. I was a member of The Dublin Typographical Provident Society or the DTPS one of the oldest unions in Ireland having been formed in 1809. My grandfather Michael O'Flanagan was elected General secretary of this union in 1913 during the Great Lockout. He remained in that position until 1920 seeing the union through one of the most turbulent times in Irish history. There were five unions in Dollards, the DTPS, The Irish Transport and General Workers Union, The Women Workers Union, The Bookbinders Union, and the Sterotypers' Union. I had no sooner started my apprenticeship than the printers went on strike. The strike lasted ten weeks after which the employers agreed to one pound a week by way of a pay rise. Even at that stage I observed that it would take three years for the members to recover the pay they lost during the ten week strike. This strike didn't affect me all that much but two other strikes that occurred at that time had a much greater affect on me. The Bank strike resulted in me being paid in Scottish and English pound notes which many shops refused to accept. Worse still was the bus strike which curtailed all forms of entertainment and forced me to repair several bicycle punctures in order to to get to work without having to walk from Walkinstown to Essex street. Apart from printing the postcards Dollards printed a number of other items of historical significance. Among these were The Capuchin Annuals, the Sweeps-takes Tickets and Ireland's premier magazine , Ireland of the Welcomes. .I worked on all these products including on the numbering the Sweeps-stakes tickets. After a seven year apprenticeship I took my "Final Declaration" and became a fully time-served and qualified printer. This required me to make a declaration in front of the National Executive of the DTPS that I would remain loyal to the union and abide by all the rules, regulations, instructions and practices of the union so help me God.

Helena

I first saw Helena in the National Stadium when Skid Row were playing support to Fleetwood Mac. I didn't speak to her on that occasion, she was speaking to Brush Shiels and other members of the band, but she caught my eye. I also saw her in St. Gabriel's, a local dance hall on the north side of the city and spoke to her briefly.

Helena, her cousin Annie Holden and Mrs. McCaffrey

Then Brush Shiel's introduced me to her in the Town and Country Club. This was shortly before the band left for England. Helena was a fan of Skid Row and she was collecting photographs of the band. Nobody better than me to provide them. I asked her out with the promise of photographs and she invited me up to meet her in Cabra. I met her on the bridge. I was expecting her to be all dolled up to meet me but no, she arrived in a pair of football boots. Nevertheless

I cajoled her to meet me again and I brought her to the Savoy Cinema in O'Connell Street. We got into a regular pattern of going to the Cinema, In those days cinema's were packed and ushers might

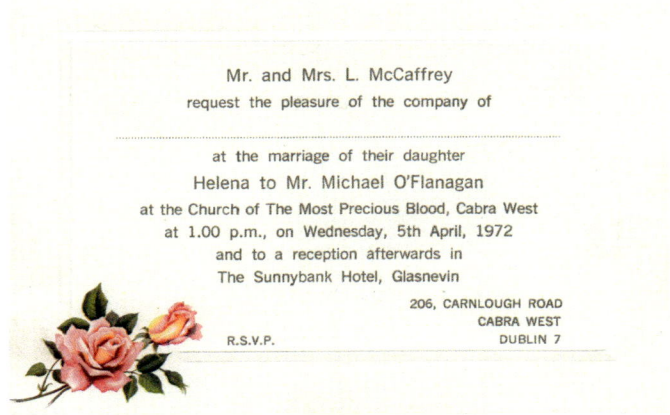

refuse you entry on spurious grounds so I used to book seats in advance. There was a risk in this in that if you were stood up you were left with two tickets. I don't remember any touts around in those days. We were very fond of the Capital Cinema and this was a place where you had to book because they showed great films and

were always in demand. On one occasion Helena's brother Patrick was sitting behind us scrutinising our carry on. He commented afterwards that we hadn't seen much of the film. We often went for something to eat after the film but Helena had a curfew, and her Dad insisted that she be home on the last bus. This meant that we would

go a restaurant in the new shopping centre on Phibsboro Road which specialised in fish and I still remember that they served excellent plaice. Eventually I was invited up to meet the family. Helena's father was a very strict man with an imposing countenance. He was over six feet tall and must have been amused at me being so small.

However I knew him for thirty two years and never had a dispute with him. Helena's mother was a very gentle mild mannered lady. It might have been because I was so small, she often asked me to go the shops for messages. I never noticed her asking either of Helena's brother-in-laws to go for messages but I was glad of the familiarity. I was accepted. Now we began a pattern of me leaving Helena home after shows. We occasionally went to the Olympia to see Jack Cruise or some of John B. Keane's plays. Mrs McCaffrey liked the singer Joseph Lock and I bought tickets and the three of us went together. When we arrived home after a show myself and Helena would go into the parlor for a kissing secession. That would be as far as things would go. One Christmas when we were in the parlor kissing I asked Helena to marry me in the glow of the

Christmas Tree. I can't remember if she said yes but from that point on we were heading in that direction. I brought her into McDowell's in O'Connell Street to buy her an engagement ring. I had saved up the money but shortly before this I had bought a harmonium and this left me with less that anticipated. Helena liked a ring which cost slightly more than I could afford and instead she settled for second

The graduations clockwise: Darragh, Ferga, Ciara and Ruadhan

best. I have often thought this was symbolic because I might have been second best myself. Anyway, though the ring was very beautiful and my two daughters are always making claims on it the incident still doesn't go unremarked all these years alter. The ring is still there but the harmonium is long gone. I found my uncle Desmond dead in my grandfather's house in late 1971. He was an unusual man with a wonderful talent for music. He was also a pioneer in colour photography, developing his own colour photographs. When he died myself and my brother Brian moved into the house. I secured the tenancy in conjunction with my aunt Eileen who had been confined to hospital for many years. When myself and Helena got married we would take Eileen out of the hospital for weekends to give her a break from her routine but she required constant medication and medical supervision. At last myself and Helena agreed on a date for our wedding. It was to be the 5th of April

The family at the launch of my book on Drimnagh Castle 2012

1972. This was an important date because it was the last day of the tax year. If you got married on that date you could claim a tax rebate for your spouse for a whole year. In effect it doubled your tax allowance for that year. It may have been because of the marriage bar that existed at that time but everyone I knew of was clued into it and nearly all availed of it. Since then Helena gave me four lovely children and a lovely life. I have loved her since the first day I saw her in the National Stadium all those years ago. We have had our rows, nearly all of which I have lost and I wouldn't claim to be the best husband in the world. Indeed many have pitied her for being married to me and Gerry Adams always commiserates with her for being lumbered with me but I have to be grateful to her for allowing me to do the things I've done and achieve the things I have achieved during our forty six years together.

RUSSELL & BERNE

Bertrand Russell introduced me to philosophy. I had read several of his books before I got stuck into his History of Western Philosophy. One of the earliest books by Russell that I enjoyed was "The Conquest of Happiness" In this book he surveyed different nationalities and pointed out why their different attitudes to life made them more happy than others. He noticed that primitive societies were likely to be happier than more sophisticated societies because they had less to worry them. He didn't recommend that we should return to primitive life styles but that we learn from their less caring attitudes. Likewise in his "In Praise of Idleness" he brought forth similar idea's. He maintained that art and culture are the products having a lot of free time or being idle. His "A Freeman's

Worship" veered a lot closer to real philosophy as did his "Why I'm Not A Christian." His work in mathematics and logic is now and always has been beyond me. For me he came to life best when he explained the thinking of all the great philosophers. I've read and re-read this book several times and can quote from memory some of the most salient passages. My favourite quotation from Russell is as follows: *"That man is the product of causes which had no prevision of the end they were achieving; that his origin, his growth, his hopes and fears, his loves and his beliefs, are but the outcome of accidental collocations of atoms; that no fire, no heroism, no intensity of thought and feeling, can preserve an individual life*

beyond the grave; that all the labors of the ages, all the devotion, all the inspiration, all the noonday brightness of human genius, are destined to extinction in the vast death of the solar system, and that the whole temple of Man's achievement must inevitably be buried beneath the debris of a universe in ruins–all these things, if not quite beyond dispute, are yet so nearly certain, that no philosophy which rejects them can hope to stand. Only within the scaffolding of these truths, only on the firm foundation of unyielding despair, can the soul's habitation henceforth be safely built". I've been reading Bertrand Russell now for fifty years and his work consoles me whenever I need consolation.

Next to Russell I elevate the work of Eric Berne. Berne formulated a new style of Psychoanalysis called Transactional Analysis which envisages all humans as having split personalities. Not just two personalities but three personalities, Adult, Child and Parent. Under his system people think in one of three different moods ie. as children, as parents or as adults. The phrase "we need an adult in the room" which has become popular since Christine Le Gard uttered it during the Greek financial crisis is derived from this form of psychoanalysis. The most important aspect that I have gleaned from studying Bern's work is most people are blissfully unaware of their own motivations in speaking to or interacting with other people. Their sub-conscious drives and motivations control their conscious activity. These sub-conscious drives and motivations are not raw or innate but conditioned by early life experiences. Berne explains this best in his "Layman's Guide to Psychiatry." However what made his work most famous was his book "The Games People Play" which has sold nearly ten million copies since it was first published

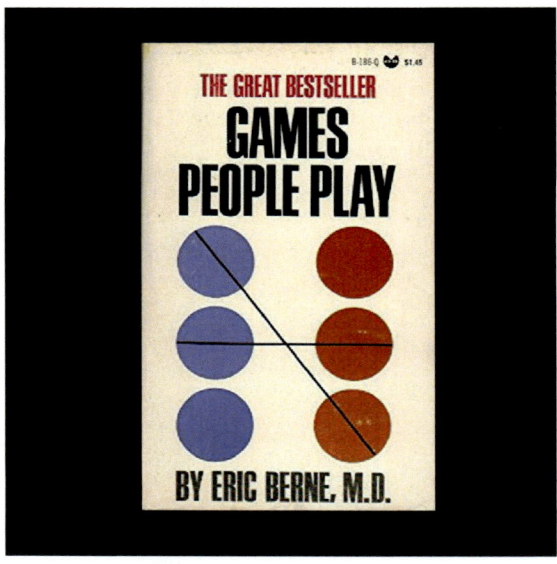

in 1964. In the first half of this book, Berne introduces transactional analysis as a way of interpreting social interactions. He describes three roles or ego states, known as the Parent, the Adult, and the Child, and postulates that many negative behaviors can be traced to switching or confusion of these roles. The second half of the book catalogues a series of "mind games" in which people interact in a patterned and predictable series of "transactions" that may appear normal to bystanders or even to the people involved, but which actually conceal motivations and lead to a well-defined predictable outcome, usually counterproductive. The book uses casual, often humorous phrases such as "See What You Made Me Do," " and "Ain't It Awful" as a way of briefly describing each game. In reality, the "winner" of a mind game is the person that returns to the Adult ego-state first.

The GO GO Club

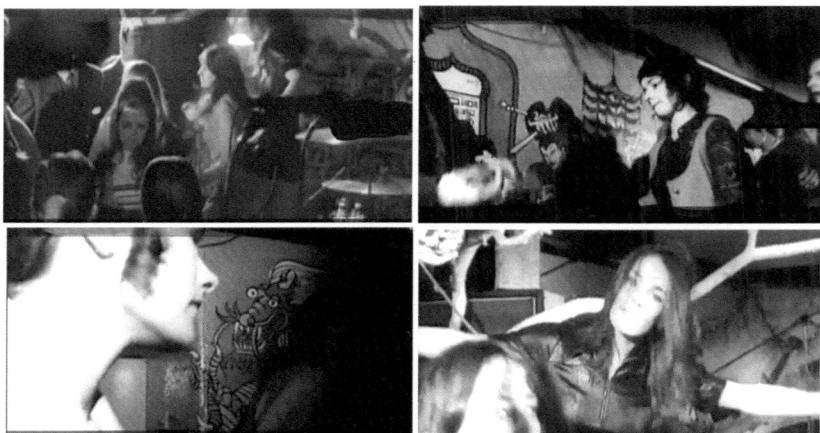

Inside the GO GO Club 1966

Yeah, I was introduced to the Go Go Club in 1965 when I worked with Tony Cullen. This was the hub of modernity at that time and although the "scene" in Dublin was very small and everyone knew everyone on the scene, the Go Go was where you were most likely to meet up. Stevie Bolger was the main DJ there and he had a huge collection of up to date music. The venue was most remarkable because of the grotesque images painted onto the stone walls of the basement in luminous paint. The young patrons were just as colourful but probably all virgins. The ceiling of the club had a series of ultra violet lights which gave everything white a penetrating sharpness so that one's skin looked show white but your freckles looked like holes in your face. Teeth could be seen sparking from ten feet away. This was definitely a place for boys to meet girls that lived in different districts of the city as opposed to going out with the girl from next door whose father knew all about you. Of course there was a huge group scene in Dublin at the time with numerous guys posing as lead singers in a band. The Go Go was a very small venue but it did feature live groups at the weekends although I doubt they were paid very much to perform. The Black Eagles never performed in the Go Go though Philip was a regular patron and I often brought him home on the back of my Honda. 50.

Bands that played there regularly were The Bye-laws, The Fix, Granny's Intentions, Some People and The Method. There was no alcohol and the fare consisted of Club Milks, Penguin Bars, Fanta Orange of Fanta Lemon. However everybody smoked although drugs were unknown in these clubs at this time. Other Clubs of significance were the Five and the Moulin Rouge. The Five was like a cavern and had a very strict membership rules because this is where the youngest teenagers were always trying to get in. Pat Egan was a guest DJ here on occasions but Tony Johnson was the regular

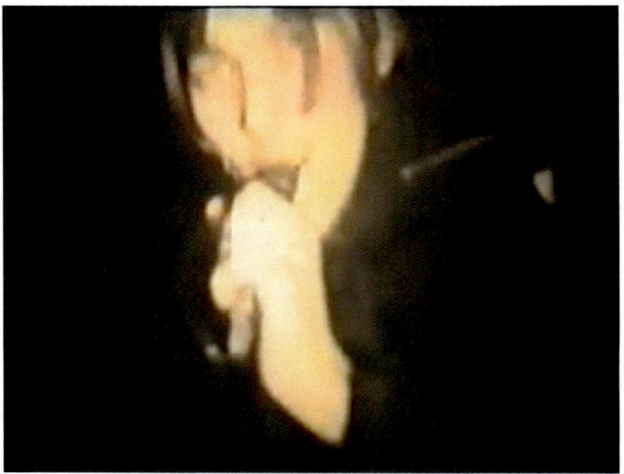

Jon Hodges hugely popular DJ in The Moulin Rouge 1969

DJ. There were no lighting effects or decorations in this club and patrons sometimes played chess or draughts on tables just inside the entrance. I bought a large Bell and Howell 35 mm projector and gave liquid light shows just to give the place some atmosphere. Again Fanta Orange or Lemon were the only drinks available. The Moulin Rouge had an older clientele. The DJ here was Jon Hodges. A very tall elegant young man he knew his music and put on a great show. Extremely popular he was close friends with Phillp Lynott and Brush Shiels. The whole scene was devastated when he died of Leukemia in 1969. The Moulin Rouge was a much larger club and featured international acts such as John Mayall, Procol Harum .and the Moody Blues. Skid Row played at this venue with both Bernard

The Five Club in Harcourt Street

The Creatures Play the Five Club

Cheevers and with Gary Moore as lead guitarists. I made movies in this club which can be viewed on Youtube. This club which was set in an old church had an eerie feel to it and it was subsequently converted into one of Dublin's first health clubs. These primitive beat clubs were condemned by the council in the early seventies and replaced with more up-market and expensive clubs such as The Countdown Club, Sloopy's, The Flamingo and Zhivago's where you could buy a bottle of wine. The Go Go fans were not happy and prepared to put up a fight. They formed an alliance and got together and made pickets and paraded up and down O'Connell Street for several Saturdays in the hope of saving their club. Sadly it was not to be. The music changed, the style changed and the clubs changed. Other venues sprung up such as the Television Club which had previously been the Four Provinces Ballroom. Such clubs were owned by wealthier proprietors who could hire several bands and DJs and provide much more plush surroundings. These venues held much larger crowds. Guest artists could enter through back doors and avoid autograph hunters so there was a lot less intimacy between the bands and the fans. The days of the beat-clubs were well and truly over.

Protesters outside the Go Go Club 1970

The Hunger-strike

Joe Cahill and Maura Drumm at the GPO, Easter 1976

When the "troubles" broke out in 1969 I was traveling in a Dublin bus with Gary Moore. We had seen the photos in the newspaper that morning and we had the first of many discussions on those events. Gary was a Presbyterian and from a unionist background. He had no interest in politics and was amazed when I told him about my days in the Fianna Eireann. He laughed when he recited the skipping rhyme sung by Catholic children in West Belast *"Jesus was born in as stable, Jesus was born in a stable, Jesus was born in a stable because the Protestants had all the houses."* I had never heard this and there was a lot I did not know about Belfast. When the band went off to England I stayed behind with my girlfriend Helena. We got married and had our family. I began working twelve hour days taking on as much overtime as I could get to pay for furniture, cots and prams. I cycled to work to save on bus fares in all weathers sometimes leaving in dark and returning in the dark. When my friend Frank Murray who traveled the world with Skid Row, Thin Lizzy, Elton John, The Pogues and even Bob Dylan met me in Dublin he was amazed at how white my skin was. He said "Mick you are as white as a sheet." That's how little sunshine I was getting. I was working in The Three Candles printing company on the morning after Bloody Sunday when thirteen people were shot in Derry by the British Army. The company allowed all the workers out for two hours to protest at the British Embassy at the killing of these innocent people. I went along with all my work mates up to the Embassy and saw that there were tens of thousands there already.

Myself and my friend Eamon Drummond decided to buy a bow and arrow. We bought it in a sports shop in Liffey Street. This was not a toy but a real bow and arrow, in fact it came with three arrows. We then bought some fire lighters which we tied to the tips of the arrows. Later that evening we returned to the Embassy with the intention of firing the arrows in through the already broken windows. We lit our arrows and took turns at firing at the windows but the wind kept blowing the arrows back into the crowds over whose heads we were trying to shoot. We failed, but the Embassy went up in flames in any case doubtless with the connivance of he Gardai probably their most patriotic moment in the thirty years of the troubles. I went back to working twelve hour days until 1976. Come Easter 1976 the Cosgrave Government banned the 60th Anniversary Easter Commemorations . My father invited me to take part in the banned Sinn Fein march from St. Stephen's Green to the GPO. It turned into the single biggest demonstration of Republicanism since 1916. People from all walks of life and from many different political backgrounds turned out to express their contempt for Cosgrave's decision. Meanwhile the political prisoners in Long Kesh had gone on the "blanket protest." The British Government had decided to remove political status from the prisoners. I decided it was time for me to join Sinn Fein. I joined the local Robert Emmet Cumann. The work associated with the Cumann was mainly selling An Phoblacht. There up to forty members of the Robert Emmet Cumman and we sold An Phoblacht from Drimnagh all the way up to Clondalkin. We also did a lot of postering and

The police beating protesters off the street in O'Connell street 1981

painting white H-Block slogans on any wall that was vacant. With my printing experience I brought out a local newsletter. I was elected Public Relations Officer for Sinn Fein in Dublin. I brought out a Newspaper called the Dublin Republican which was concerned with social issues in the Dublin area. Then the Hunger-strikes came on. Bobby Sands went on Hunger-strike on the first of March 1981. We organised protest marches in O'Connell Street every evening. When the H-Block Committee decided to run Bobby Sands in a by-election in Fermanagh South Tyrone I went up to canvas for him in the Dungannon area. I also canvassed for Paddy Agnew in Co. Louth and for Eoin Carron after Bobby Sands died. It was a very traumatic time. I spoke outside the churches in Fintona and Seskinore which were deep in the heart of Unionist territory. With the deaths of the Hunger-stikers the republican movement took to more extreme actions in the war. I was particularly distraught when they refused to condemn a no-warning bombing by the INLA in Derry. The Droppin Well bombing occurred on 6th December 1982, when the Irish National Liberation Army (INLA) exploded a time bomb at a disco in Ballykelly Co. Derry. The disco, known as the Droppin Well, was targeted because it was frequented by British Army soldiers from nearby Shackleton Barracks. The bomb killed eleven soldiers and six civilians and thirty people were injured. I wrote to the Ard Comhairle of Sinn Fein and asked them to issue a statement condemning no-warning bombs. They declined and I resigned from Sinn Fein. While accidents do happen in war, I could never countenance the deliberate killing of innocent civilians

The Frederick Press

As a journeyman printer you move around from job to job. This is a tradition in the Printing going back hundreds of years. Printers where the only tradesmen allowed to wear swords in the 1700s. This was because sometimes the things they printed could make enemies and put their lives at risk. In my time the reason for moving around from one company had a different purpose. Printing was a highly skilled job and so some printers were better than others at doing their job. If a printer made a mistake and the colour was wrong or the picture was mottled the whole product could end up in the bin and have to be re-printed at the company's expense. Some printers made less mistakes than others and these were in great demand. So when

there were vacancies a company would seek the best printers available and pay them extra money above the union rate. This was called merit money. So printers moved around from one company to another seeking higher merit money. So long as the printers kept moving the merit money got higher and higher and that's why printers kept moving around. It was for such a reason that I moved to the Frederick Press which was owned by Carroll's, the cigarette company at the time. You might wonder why a cigarette company would own a printing company but that was where they printed the cigarette cartons. One of the benefits of working for this company was that all the employees got season tickets to the Carroll's Irish Open Golf Tournament every year. From my point of view the best reason to work for this company was it enabled me to transfer from Letterpress Printing to Litho Printing. After finishing my apprenticeship in Dollards I had spent some years working in the Three Candles. This was a famous printing company owned by Colm O'Loughlin who had a television program on RTE called "Zozimus Said" Colm collected and re-printed all the old Dublin street ballads. He also printed the works of James Connolly. However all of these works were printed by letterpress, a process that was fast dying out. They new computerised composition methods allowed for much more coloured photographs to be reproduced more quickly. The litho plates could be reproduced in a method similar to printing a photograph, that is, by simply exposing the image to light. A litho-plate could be made in minutes while a similar letterpress forme would take days to make up. Also Litho machines were much faster in production. In the Frederick Press I was trained to operate both small and large Litho-press machines. These skills were in much greater demand and commanded much higher wages. As in Dollards, The Three Candles and the Frederick press I made great friends, some still alive and some since sadly long since passed away. Among those that spring to mind were John Tyrell, John Field, Paddy Richardson, Vincent Timmons, Willie Ward, Tony Cullen, Anne Leonard , Martha Ellis, Marie Bermingham, Jim Casserly from Dollards, Jack Walsh, Peter O'Leary, Jimmy Hackett, Paul Doyle, Violet Drummond, Dick O'Toole Eddie Cahill and Jjimmy Gleeson from the Three Candles, and Joe O'Sullivan, Jim Rice, Jack Doyle, Brendan Doyle, Sean Werren, Margaret Elliot, and Phyllis Lennon all from the Frederick Press. Apart from the odd row I greatly enjoyed working with all these people, spent many a Christmas party with them and occasionally played Pitch and Putt with them sometimes for charity. For many years I went fishing with Jimmy Gleeson including a trip to Black Sod Bay from where I caught a nine pound Ling, a fish very similar to a large cod. We were lucky not to be swept away by the force nine gale that day.

Fine Arts

Fine Arts was a different kettle of fish. This company had large format six-colour presses. It took four printers to operate these machines. Most of those reading this will not appreciate the importance of baseball cards to youngsters buying chewing gum in America. . This company printed these base-ball cards one hundred and forty-four up on one sheet of card. The sheets of card were six feet wide and four feet deep. A palette of card weighed several tons. It takes four colours to produce a coloured photograph but with a six-colour press you can add extra colours such as gold or silver and a varnish. This enabled vast quantities of a product to be produced in a single pass through these machines. I joined this company in 1988 and contracted to work a twelve hour day six days a week as a number two printer. Working 8am to 8pm gave me twenty-four hours overtime and enabled me to double the wages I had been earning for the previous ten years. This enabled me to re-plumb and re-wire my house. The company operated twenty-fours a day either with two twelve hour shifts or three eight hour shifts. After a year I transferred to the three shift system which gave me less money but more time with my family. Fine Arts also printed the famous Fine Art Christmas cards and cartons for ready-made meals. The workforce in this company was highly regimented following an American army style of disciple which was necessary to maximise production.

Conscience, Destiny and Choice.

I had been made redundant for the first time circa Christmas 1991 when I decided put an idea which had been playing on my mind for a number of years into action. Being mindful of the work of several of Russell's recommended philosophers I had been pondering the concepts of Conscience, Destiny and Choice. I conceived a method to portray these concepts in a work of art. Living within three hundred yards of the Irish Museum of Modern Art I had witnessed some very odd phenomena posing as art. Like black squares in the middle of an otherwise white canvas or floors covered with spilt rice The question was: who was fooling who? Nothing meant nothing and still nothing was appreciated. I set about producing a work of art

With Karl Judge in Kimainham Gaol 1994

that would have meaning and at the same time would give extra meaning to everyday items. Installations were all the rage with pieces of fat or old cigarette butts being displayed in glass bowls and being celebrated as major innovations. I was determined that my piece would be more accessible. I decided to put together an installation made from household items but finished to make a highly polished presentation. I spent six months working on the items, polishing, painting and gluing them together so as to make a display that would shine and at the same time speak to the sub-conscious. The Conscience piece was circle of wooden spoons faced with the ten commandments featuring a clock with a ticking second-hand pointing alternatively to each of the commandments in turn. The Destiny piece was a similar circle of wooden spoons faced the Tarot cards again with a similar clock pointing alternatively to each card combining both the moment and the shock of sudden surprise that accompanies each moment. Finally I laid out a highly polished table laid flat on the floor without any legs and set with twelve small bowels filled with different coloured substances and again with a ticking clock pointing alternatively to each bowel which challenged the viewer to choose one of the bowels and the substance therein. These substances were labeled as emotions such as love, hatred, fear anger etc. Apart from the beauty of the items on display and the concepts they portrayed the ticking clocks gave the installation an animated feel to it. Helen O'Donoghue who was community liaison officers with IMMA offered to put the work on show in the gallery in partnership with an American artist who like myself had made her art out of household objects. However this offer fell through although the American artist's show did go ahead and was a great success. Nevertheless this left me without a venue to put my piece on show. There was a waiting list of up to three years for artists to get space in the scarce art galleries in Dublin. Luckily for me I discovered that there was an artists co-operative in St. Mary's Church in Wolfe Tone Street. It was housed in the church that Wolfe Tone himself was baptised in. For a small fee I became a member of the co-operative and prepared to take part in their quarterly group show. I photographed the work from every angle and sent it Patrick Gallagher with an explanation of the rationale behind the work. This was a crazy thing to do. Established high profile artists occasionally get their work reviewed in obscure publications but only with the help of agents and PR firms. For a novice to get a review in a National Newspaper was unheard of. But I struck the jackpot. Mr. Gallagher, art critic of the Sunday Independent published a glowing review of my work in the following Sunday's paper. Meanwhile I made a friend of Karl Judge who was a prolific artist and who gave me excellent advice on several aspects of the art business. Together we subsequently staged a very large communal art exhibition in Kilmainham Gaol in 1994. Karl also illustrated my poetry book.

Sunday Independent 3rd May 1992

Druids in the galleries

ART — Patrick Gallagher

ART can be a puzzling business. Consider two exhibitions in Dublin, Michael O'Flanagan's in St. Mary's Church beyond Arnotts and Wolfgang Laib's in the Douglas Hyde Gallery. One is in a dilapidated church in a shabby street, the other in a fine gallery in an ancient university. One artist exhibits all over the world, the other is known only in a suburb of his native city.

The two men have a good deal in common despite the very different status they are given in the art business as it is currently structured. The Irishman is 43, the German 42. Neither set out to be an artist. O'Flanagan is a Dublin artisan who trained as and still is a printer. Laib is a German bourgeois who qualified as a doctor but never practised. By way of information one exhibition provides a single sheet of paper, the other a fine colour catalogue.

There may not be a great deal to choose between the two. That is not to say either is a bad artist, in fact it is quite probable that both of them are good artists. It is merely to draw attention to the fact that what is shared between them has little to do with art and a great deal to do with religion or holding a set of values or a sense of otherness.

If these two men are simply "religious" men performing sacramental or religious rites in art galleries (and that is what they seem to be doing) can we describe them as being artists at all? Might they not belong to a category of priests or druids or mystic facilitators?

Mick O'Flanagan faced up to that problem in his opening speech when he told his friends from Inchicore that they were entitled to wonder was he a megalomaniac or did he have emotional problems. He quite obviously hasn't. The assemblage he shows is made from ordinary kitchen objects — wooden spoons, bread boards and so on. It represents three concepts important to him — conscience, destiny and choice. A circle of ordinary wooden spoons looks inward. The bowl of each spoon is inscribed with one of the ten commandments and the Sacred Heart of Jesus is on the eleventh spoon. That represents conscience. Destiny is shown by the court cards of a deck on another circle of spoons presided over by the Joker. And coloured tubs of paint represent all the emotions, the element of choice. It is a strong, naive and touching installation, tribal art of our time, something to do with the moral joustings now affecting our whole community.

THE single and disappointing square of pollen shown by Wolfgang Laib in the second exhibition is a sort of votive offering to something — perhaps to ecological metaphysics or to the Eastern Sufism he absorbed in his father's village hospital in India. Mick O'Flanagan told his friends anybody could do what he has done in St. Mary's Church but the whole glitzy apparatus of galleries and artspeak hides the fact that anyone can also do what Laib has done.

He just gathers pollen from pine trees in jars and sieves it onto the floor. His materials, like O'Flanagan's, are everyday things. He gathers the sulphur-like pollen as it falls from the male catkins in the forest. This is how he lives, exhibiting pollen — or on other occasions milk or beeswax — and offering them to his god. Is his deity a cleverly-concealed god of Mammon or is he returning all things to a traditional god?

Many of us could easily copy what O'Flanagan and Laib do, and O'Flanagan actually encourages us to do just that. So are these men artists or priests? There is a clue in the Laib catalogue where it quotes the mystical friar Meister Eckhart, who speculated that art simply was religion — and religion art. Today he might speculate about one ordinary Dub and one fashionable European.

Conscious, Destiny and Choice in St. Mary's Church 1992

The Inchicore and Kilmainham Development Project.

It was originally intended to have the Single European Act. ratified by the end of 1986. Eleven of the twelve member states of the EEC had already ratified the treaty. The deadline failed to be achieved however when the Irish government were restrained from ratifying the treaty pending court proceedings brought by my good friend Raymond Crotty. In the court case, the Irish Supreme Court ruled that the Irish Constitution would have to be amended before the

state could ratify the treaty, something that can only be done by referendum. The referendum was ultimately held on 26 May 1987 and the proposal was approved by Irish voters and Ireland formally ratified the Single European Act in June 1987, allowing the treaty to come into force on 1st July. 1987. Mr. Haughey was the Taoiseach at the time and he was mighty relieved. What swung the referendum was Mr. Haughey's promise that Ireland would benefit greatly from the newly established "Cohesion Funds." Some eleven billion was set aside to iron out the disparities between the poorer countries on the periphery of the EEC and the richer countries at the centre. This allowed for millions to be drawn down from Eurpoe for local development in Ireland. However that came with certain conditions. Proper local structures had to be in place to carry out local planning and to receive the money. So it was that all over Ireland new Local Development Projects were set up. We in Inchicore set up The Inchicore and Kilmainham Development Project. Over a two year

Mary O'Rouke, Alison Madock , Gwen Doyle and Eadaoin Ni Clearaigh

period the group met in the priests house and the parish priest Fr. Michael O'Connor acted as our chairman. The group consisted of the Family Resource Centre, the Youth Project, the Grand Canal Group, local school teachers. local historians and I was there as the editor of a small local newspaper The Inchicore Times. As a background to this I must point out that when I launched The Inchicore Times I envisaged that the area would benefit from having a quarterly newspaper devoted to recording the happenings in the local area. Indeed many country towns with smaller populations than Inchicore had sustained local newspapers for decades without difficulty. At first I had no difficulty in getting advertisments to finance the publication but it soon became clear that the local shops and businesses could not afford to pay for advertising more than once a year. This gave an accurate picture of how depressed the village of Inchicore was. All the more reason to set up a

Development Project. The group was lucky to have two historians on board, Seosamh O Broin who had spent fifty years compiling a book which was subsequently published under the title Inchicore, Kilmainham and District and Cllr. Michael Conaghan who published a series of magazines also recording the history of our illustrious area. We also had artists, architects, botanists and poets in the group. The group drew up a plan for the re-development of the area under the title "Realising Potential." This had chapters and proposals on high-lighting employment creating opportunities in the natural environment, the village heritage, the architecture of the area, the mills in the area, the industrial heritage of the area, local culture and the arts, a proposed craft centre and the archaeology of the area. The plan was launched in The Royal Hospital Kilmainham in July 1990 with Minister Mary O'Rourke as a guest. The meeting was chaired by Gwen Doyle and the main speaker was Fr. Michael O'Connor. RTE covered the event and I was interviewed on the One O'Clock News. We made a case for Inchicore and Kilmainham to be included in the Government's proposed new Partnership Area's . It was through this mechanism that the Cohesion Funds were to be

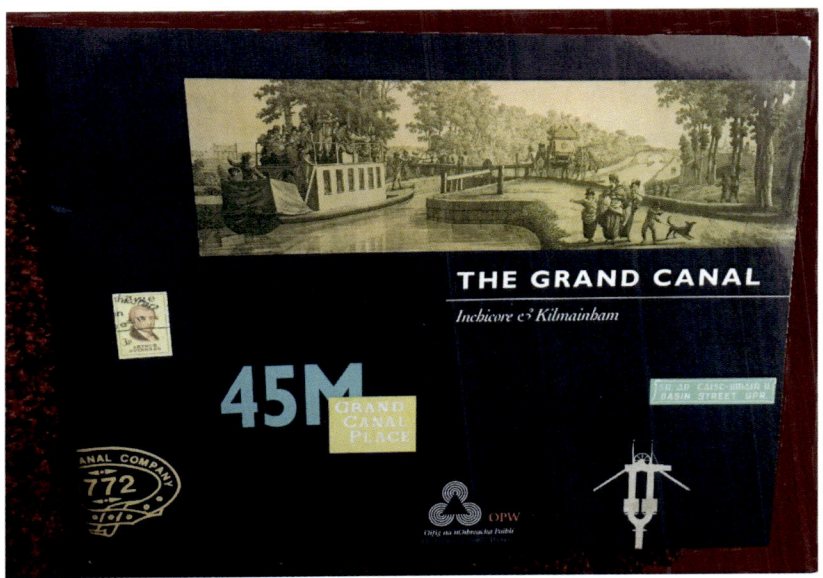

disbursed Interviewed on the News Minister O'Rourke said how impressed she was by the work we had done and was sure we would be included in the partnership scheme. However, within weeks we discovered we had missed out because "our area was too small." Two years later when Jim Mitchell TD and his brother Gay Mitchell were in government and the Inchicore area was amalgamated with the Rialto area under the title The Canals Community Partnership

Syllables

I had been writing poetry since I was seventeen years old. I used to think up my rhyming verses as I took my Sunday morning walks up to the Greenhills and back down to the Submarine bar. I was influenced by Robert Graves and James Clarence Mangan. So when I worked in O'Sullivan Print about 1990 I arranged to have my book printed where I worked. I chose a very unusual size because it would be most economically produced in that size allowing sixteen pages to be printed on one side of the sheet of paper and sixteen more pages on the other side of the sheet. This meant that the whole book could be printed on one sheet of paper and with only two printing plates. The poems themselves were juvenile as I had nothing to compare them with having never participated in a workshop. However I now needed an audience and a venue to launch my new poetry book. Phillis McGuirk who was a fellow member of the Inchicore and Kilmainham Development Project told me that Liam O'Meara had a poetry group called Syllables and she was a member. I arranged to meet Liam and told him that I had arranged to launch my poetry book in the Patriot Inn and I would welcome his members to come along and to read their poems at the event. This worked a treat and Liam then invited me to join the Syllables Group. The group met every Sunday evening in the Priest's House in Inchicore at 7pm. The idea was that each member would read a new poem or a piece that they were working on and the other members would then offer comments, suggestions, or criticisms of the new work. The comments and suggestions were always a great help but the criticisms sometimes didn't go down so well. In my own case I had a large number of poems written over a period 20 years and I wasn't inclined to start re-writing them. Also the more modern style familiar to the group was less than familiar to me. However after a

while I began to appreciate the freedom of the modern style and the wider range of possible expression that it engendered. Liam O'Meara was widely read and had a collection of first editions of some of the most classical of books. He could discuss the work of numerous authors and was familiar with all the classics. So it was that my own work improved rapidly in this atmosphere. The group occasionally published slim volumes of the members work and these were produced economically and sold to local supporters of the group. I contributed three poems to the Syllables Third Anthology. This was launched in the Patriot Inn by the late Jim Mitchell TD who was very fond Liam O'Meara's poems and sometimes included them in his Christmas Cards. The Syllables Group also organised an annual poetry competition. I developed a close friendship with Liam which led to many other projects over the following twenty-five years

The Constitution Club

Desmond Fennell invited me to join his newly formed Constitution Club in 1986. He formed seven man executive committee to establish the Club and they appointed me secretary. My duties were to keep minutes of the meetings and ensure proper communication with all the members. The purpose of the Club was to examine in which way the Irish Constitution could be improved taking into account that 1987 would mark it's fiftieth anniversary. The Club was primarily concerned with the mechanisms of government rather than crude political disputes. The idea was to invite persons with new idea's from different disciplines to give papers on a monthly basis in a central venue and invite audiences who could appreciate the topics and who could critique them with a sufficient degree of expertise. The committee was composed as follows Tom Barrington

Desmond Fennell, Raymond Crotty, John Robb and Donal Barrington.

founder of the Institute of Public Administration who had written an important book on the need for decentralisation of government. He was the chair of the committee. Next was Senator John Robb from Ballymoney, Dr. Roy Johnson of Trinity College, John Rodden , Donal O'Brollachain who held posts in the Civil Service, myself and finally Mr. Raymond Crotty an agricultural economist from Trinity College who had written a hugely important book entitled "Ireland in Crisis: A Study in Capitalist Colonial Undevelopment." The Club held it's meetings in Buswell's Hotel on the first Tuesday of every month, I took the minutes and sent out a monthly newsletter to all members who paid an annual subscription of £5. The first paper presented to the inaugural meeting of the Constitution Club, in Buswell's Hotel, on November 5th 1986, by Dr Roy Johnston was entitled 'Innovation, Employment and Regional Government' in which he made a case for building regional governmental structures

around the existing distribution of regional colleges. This attracted support from a lot of people critical of the over-centralist structure of the State, as inherited from the British imperial model. Membership of the Club grew to about one hundred and twenty and included such notables as Michael McDowell, Anthony Coughlin, Sean Dublin Bay Loftus,, Fr. Sean Healey, Carmencita Hedderman, PJ. Power, and Rosemary Rowley. Papers were given by Dr. Donal Barrington, Ray McSharry, Michael McDowell, Raymond Crotty, John Rodden, and I gave a paper myself on the Case for a Citizen's Initiative, that is, that ordinary people should be enabled to initiate laws or call referendums by collecting 100,000 signatures. I also proposed that Dail constituencies should be single seater constituencies and that political parties should be disbarred from holding seats on local councils. While a lot of very valuable discussion took place, the news media gave the Club very little oxygen and it's influence failed to extend beyond the walls of Buswell's Hotel. Unfortunately, it wound up in 1989 without securing any changes to the 1937 Constitution

Michael Hartnett

Michael Hartnett reciting his poem at the Patriot Inn 1992

I became acquainted with Michael Hartnett through Liam O'Meara and the Syllables writers' group. Liam had been awarded a poetry prize in a competition judged by Michael and Liam had made a large poster of Michael's Inchicore Haiku poem and installed it on the wall of McDowell's pub in Inchicore. Then when the Syllables group held poetry readings in The Patriot Inn Michael used to invite himself along and join in the poetry recitals willy nilly as was his wont. When myself and Liam decided to set-up the Inchicore Ledwidge Society we invited Michael to be our guest of honour at our inaugural event in the National War Memorial Park in 1995. Michael had a great love for Inchicore having come here after his marriage breakup in 1985. He was driven up from Limerick in the depths of winter by his friend Charlie Lodge. Michael lived in several different locations in Inchicore over ten years but his favourite haunt was McDowell's pub on Emmet Road. He bought a copy of An Phoblacht from me every week as he sat at the bar beside the old fashioned snug. He had great sympathy for the Hunger-strikers and wrote a poem called "Who Killed Bobby Sands." He was a fluent Irish speaker having learned the language from his granny in Newcastle West in Limerick. He translated the great Irish poets of the eighteenth century into English. He had a ready wit and was always great fun to be with. When I was giving a poetry reading in the Patriot Inn he kept interrupting me in both Irish and English. When I launched my poetry broadsheet Riposte he was amongst the first of the established poets to give it his imprimatur.

He gave me several poems for publication which gave Riposte credibility in the eyes of other subscribing poets. I often talked to him on the phone and he would leave the phone to go and light his cigarette from his gas cooker. He was a very delicate little man and those of us who knew him were constantly worried about him especially when he had too much drink taken. I made a video of him reading in the Patriot Inn which can be viewed on Youtube. In September 1999 he rang me at 8am on a Sunday morning and asked me to republish his Inchicore Haiku and to dedicate it to his best friend Charlie Lodge who had just died. I immediately set about this task but God spoke before us all. Myself and Liam O'Meara had organised a major re-launch of Michael's work and his career in McDowell's pub where he had written many of the Haiku when the news came that he himself had died on 13th October 1999. Michael was one of Ireland's most important poets who was unfortunately over shadowed by lesser poets towards the end of his life when the fashion in poetry changed and Art's Council's favourites took over.

Peep into the Abyss

Syllables had previously held a number of poetry readings in the Patriot Inn and we had launched two anthologies when I gathered together a collection of my later poems. I was going through a particularly bad patch in terms of stress when these poems were written. Everything looked black. Meanwhile Liam O'Meara also had a collection of his work ready for publication. I called my book Peep into the Abyss and Liam called his book Guardians of the Poem. We were lucky to have Karl Judge on hand to illustrate both books. We decided to have both books printed simultaneously and jointly launched. What was most advantageous to us was that the

Brendan Kennelly, Leo McCaffrey, Michael O'Flanagan and Liam O'Meara reading in the Black Lion Pub in 1994

Printing firm I worked for was specialising in digital print. This was a totally new innovation in print at a time when we were still typesetting our chap-books on typewriters. Unlike traditional printing methods this method required no plate making apparatus. Whole books could be produced one at a time. This meant that it was economical to order a hundred books or even less. The cost of each individual book remained the same however many were printed as there were no set-up costs as with traditional printing. I had the bright idea of inviting Brendan Kennelly to launch our books and we booked the function room in the Black Lion Pub in Inchicore for the book launch. I wrote to Professor Kennelly in Trinity College sending him samples of our work including photographs of Karl Judge's paintings. It was our total naivety that resulted in our success. Not only did Professor Kennelly launch our books in great style but he gave us glowing tributes for the quality of our work. He

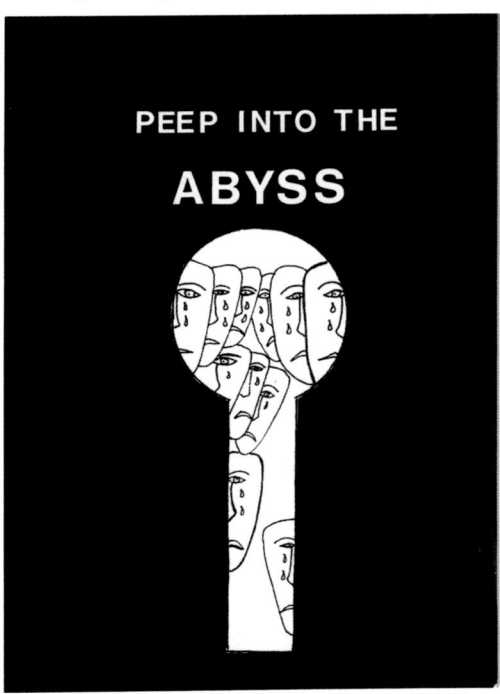

wrote a commendation for Liam's book which he was subsequently was able to use in furtherance of his many future publications. Above all Brendan thoroughly enjoyed the occasion and vowed to return again to to read his own work in Inchicore. I became firm friends with Brendan and he supported and subscribed to Riposte for twenty years. He was glad to have several of his poems featured in editions of the broadsheet over the years

The Shuffling Feet on the Stairs

Leo McCraffrey polishing his shoes before going to work 1960

On the night of the book launch in the Black Lion my father-in-law Mr. Leo McCaffrey gave a rendition of his favourite poem the Shuffling Feet on the Stairs. Leo was 86 years old at the time and never fluffed a line of this epic. He had come across it in Ireland's Own decades before, he learned off by heart and would recite it on any occasion, weddings, christenings or even at funerals. Professor Kennelly was mightily impressed as he loved anything that reflected or portrayed the character and traits of old Dubliners

Shuffling Feet on the Stairs.

In a tenement house in an old city street
In squalor and grime but content
That was marred once a week when the landlord
 Came round to collect his few shillings of rent

Lived half dozen families
and many more
with a tap on each landing supplying their need

and the door-knocker pinched from the door.
They were all friends in need when old trouble came round
Between times they might have their fights
And they borrowed and pawned for the rest of the week
for a hooley on Saturday night.

Twas a communal life with no secrets to hide
And all knew each others affairs
With one big exception, the man that they called
The shuffling feet on the stairs.

None knew from where he came ; none knew his name
He lived in the attic above
There were those who had met him and bid him good-day
but these he pushed past with a shove.

These people would tell you that the fellow was old
Dark-browed and powerfully built
that he walked with a limp like a man with a great load
of guilt.

But most of the tenants ne'er saw him at all
For he rarely went out until night.
And sometimes at midnight you'd hear him come home
And sometimes at dawn's early light

But sometimes it was early and he coming home
With the families all still at their prayers
And the children would cry in their fright when they heard
The shuffling feet on the stairs.

And the whole house would listen in tension and fear
As he dragged up the steps to his room
With his clumping and dragging and shuffling step
Made them feel they were waiting for doom.

And sometimes he'd switch on the light in his room
And give out a terrible roar,
Then they'd hear him go in

And they'd hear the key in his door.
And those that lived under would tell that for hours
The man would be walking the floor
with his shuffling step up and down the boards
and again and again he would roar.

There were notes to the landlord to have him put out
for the people were all now afraid
But the landlord replied that he would not evict
the one man whose rent was full paid.

Well the tension was growing and the people were going
until one night there was no sound at all
no fumbling key in the door of the house
no shuffling step in the hall.

The silence was eerie and people were weary
counting sheep in their pairs
but none could find sleep as they listened in vain
for the shuffling feet on the stairs.

That night, and the next there was no sound at all
they should have been glad it had ceased
but there's no peace for tenement dwellers
when they feel a neighbour's in trouble uneased.

So they sent for the guards and the guards broke in his room
the old man lay there on his bed
with a picture before him
a smile on his face and he dead.

Then the story came out that this man had been rich
with a mansion and servants and all
and how he'd been driving his motor one night
and he coming home from a ball

He'd had too much to drink, but didn't much care
at driving he felt he was skilled
Then the car had crash, he injured his leg

but his lovely young wife, she was killed.

He had drunk to forget until he spent all his fortune
he had drunk to forget all his tears
and from mansion to tenement from riches to poverty
this was the path of his years.

And he who had once had been a great public man
and an expert on world affairs
had sunk to the point where the one name he had
was the shuffling feet on the stairs.

Twas a Thursday they took him below to the church
where the neighbours all gathered around
as they carried the coffin below to the landing
my old ears detected a sound.

It was not the sound of the old women praying
It was not the sound of their prayers
The sound that I heard as they bore him away
Was the shuffling feet on the stairs.

The Dublin '98 Committee

I had spent two years reading about the 1798 Rebellion when it was advertised that a public meeting would be held in the Tailor's Hall to prepare for the bi-centennial commemorations of the Rebellion. I was determined to be involved and arrived early at the meeting. The

meeting was chaired by Richard Roche who was also organising the Wexford commemorations of the event. The chief guest was Avril Doyle TD and Minister. The ambition of those present was to get funding for a series of events. Minister Doyle pointed out that most of her budget was committed to the commemoration of the Famine which would also be marked in 1998. What was odd about this was that the Irish government had not bothered to mark the Famine in 1948 which would have been the hundred anniversary of Black '48. It was also suspected that the government was nervous of commemorating the Rebellion while the troubles in the north were still in full swing. This was confirmed when the Minister said that any funding for our commemorations would be contingent on not using The Pike as our symbol. This didn't go down to well with anyone in the room. It was further enforced when the National Museum announced plans to turn Croppy's Acre into a bus park just in time for the anniversary. Members of the committee included myself, Thomas MacGiolla, Aengus O'Snodaigh, Tom Stokes, Dick Roche, ,Brian Cleary, Derrick Warfield and Tommy Graham. Aengus launched a campaign which was successful in preventing Croppy's acre being converted to a bus park. However when the renovation of the park was completed is was composed of a series of large flat slabs embedded in the grass and devoid of any inscription

Unveiling the plaque   Donal Barrington, Susan Denham& Canon Pierpoint

which would give any idea that it represented the graves of hundreds of rebels hanged in 1798. Another expenditure of money supposedly to mark the Rebellion was a small park opened opposite Christchurch which featured no statuary or inscriptions. Meanwhile I was detailed to have some plaques erected to mark some of the places connected with the Rebellion in Dublin. I approached Dublin Tourism who had the authority to put up plaques in Dublin. I was told that they had a policy of not erecting plaques to "religious or political figures." To coin a phrase "they were implacable to putting up these plaques." I contacted the Minister for Tourism Jim McDaid who intervened and reversed this nonsensical policy. I eventually got plaques put on the house in Thomas street where lord Edward Fitzgerald was captured shortly before the rebellion after hiding out successfully in the Liberties for three months. I also had a plaque put up on St. Werburg's Church where he was buried. I also had a plaque put up St. Michan's Church where the Sheares Brothers were laid to rest after their execution in Newgate Prison. I also organised a commemoration concert in the Guinness Hopstore headed by singer

Frank Harte at which Minister Seamus Brennan spoke, gave us his full support and commended the group on the work achieved. The key event of the commemoration was the march past of the Pikemen who marched from the Garden of Remembrance down O'Connell street and all the way up the Quay's to Croppy's Acre.

Later that year I was invited to give a lecture on Thomas Russell in the Royal Hospital Kilmainham. The President, Mary McAleese invited . our group up to meet her in Aras An Uachtaran towards the end 1998

When They Followed Henry Joy

I had been a member of the Syllables Poetry group for a number of years when in 1995 I got the notion that I should try to write an epic poem on Henry Joy McCracken. After all Brendan Kennelly had

Tony Gregory launches When They Followed Henry Joy in Tailors Hall

written two epic poems one Judas and the other on Cromwell. I reasoned that it couldn't be that hard, it would need a little research and some determination. I first got myself a readers ticket for The National Library and began to read "The Lives of The United Irishmen" by RR. Madden. This was a very enjoyable experience. However writing the poem was less than pleasant. When I had about one hundred lines written I realised that the task was way beyond my capability. The kind of poetry that I could write was concerned with nuance and not with narrative. I was prepared to totally abandon the whole idea when Christine Broe suggested that I write McCracken's biography instead. This was an inspired idea because no substantial biography of McCracken had been written. A small pamphlet on Henry Joy McCracken had been published by The Irish News in 1967 to mark the bi-centenary of his birth but it ran to a mere sixty pages. So I tackled this secondary task with more gusto. This involved me spending two years visiting the National Library, The The Gilbert Library, The Linenhall Library and Trinity College in search of letters and references to Henry Joy McCracken. My sons Darragh and Ruadhan had recently acquired an up-to-date computer and they showed me how format the text. The book was ready for publication but I had no colour image of Henry Joy to grace the cover. Using the black and white engraved image from Dr. Madden's book I proceeded to try my hand at painting a portrait of Henry Joy McCracken with Kilmainham Gaol in the background, the relevance being that he had spent two years in the Gaol. I then installed this image on the cover of the book and sent the lo t to the printer. No

Inside the Tailor's Hall 1997

difficulties were encountered in the production of this book, something that amazes me now having had twenty years of difficulties with printers and other publishers ever since. Now all I needed was avenue to launch the book and an audience to buy it. Luckily for me I had made the acquaintance of Frank Connolly the manager of the Tailor's Hall and a stalwart of the Dublin '98 Committee. He agreed to host the launch in the very hall where Wolfe Tone had founded the United Irishmen in Dublin in 1795.I approached Tony Gregory TD to launch the book and he was delighted to be asked. He was very nervous and told me he had never launched a book before. Launching the book he said that he was immediately impressed by the concise clarity of style of the writing making the book so easy to read. The launch was a great success and I immediately got an order from an American distributor for two hundred copies of the book and they facilitated the shipping of the book to the USA. It was also reviewed favourably in their

Scenes from the play : Lord Cornwallis receives reports of the battles of 1798 and Mary Ann McCracken visits Henry Joy in Kilmainham Gaol.

publication and in the Irish Times. By now we were into 1998 and the bi-centenary of the Rebellion was in full swing. My book was considered suitable as the basis for a play by Rosin Flood, entitled Hope and Glory which was performed in Kilmainham Gaol to mark the occasion. The play which ran for two weeks, attracted large audiences, was filmed and recorded and can be viewed on Youtube. The book is still in print and I sold the painting to Charles Haughey.

Aengus O'Snodaigh and Sinn Fein

Aengus O'Snodaigh, Gerry Adams, Eamonn MacThomais and Derrick Warfield at my book launch in the Richmond House Inchicore in 2002

Having worked with Aengus O'Snodaigh on the Dublin '98 Committee I was hugely impressed by his drive and his considered judgement on the numerous issues that we encountered. When he was chosen by Sinn Fein to contest the by-election in Dublin South Central in 1999, I offered to assist him in the campaign. It was his first time to contest a Dail seat and he came very close taking the seat but was just piped by Mary Upton who was running for the Labour Party in a seat that became vacant by the death of her brother Pat Upton. I was very familiar with the constituency having been election agent for Michael O'Mahony who had run for Sinn Fein in the local elections of 1979. I greatly enjoyed the campaign for Aengus and built up a great comradery with him and his crew during the campaign. Unfortunately the poet Michael Hartnett died during the campaign and I was involved in publishing his book Inchicore Haiku. After this I joined Aengus on a number of EU referendum campaigns and found that he was a terrific campaigner Three years later in the general election of 2002 Aengus was again the Sinn Fein candidate in Dublin South Central and I again gave him my full support. He received a hugely warm reception at the doors. He had the area plastered with posters and a determined crew out night after night making the case for his election. Then a problem arose. Sinn Fein found it impossible to obtain a venue to

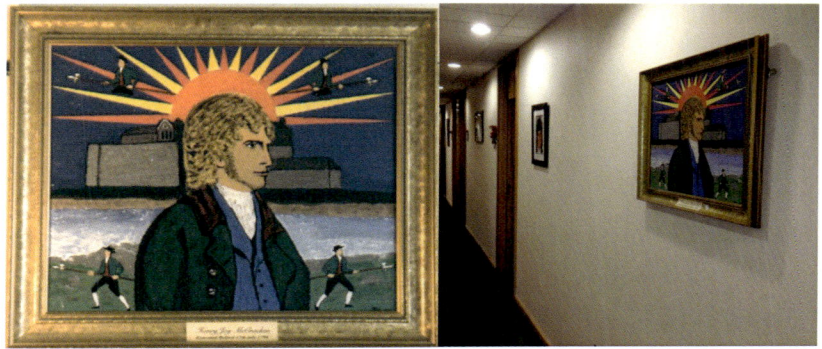

hold a final election rally. Election rallies were considered an important factor in generating momentum in the final days of election campaigns. So I offered to launch a book I had ready for publication in 2003 to mark bi-centenary of Robert Emmet' Rebellion in 1803. By this time I had published a number of books

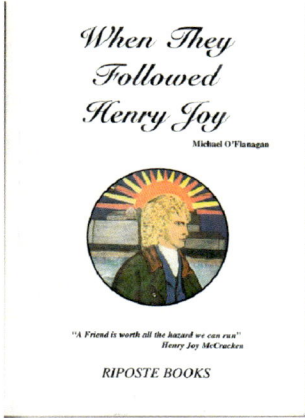

and could stage a book launch with little effort I asked Pat Ward of the Richmond House if I could launch the book in his very large pub. He agreed and I then invited Gerry Adams to launch the book. He agreed and we sent out hundreds of invitations to attend the launch and huge numbers turned up and the book launch became in effect an election rally for Aengus. Three days later the election took place and Aengus took one of two seats in Dublin for Sinn Fein for the first time since the 1920s. The book which I had written and ready for this occasion was entitled Emmet, Hope and Russell. I had written my biography of Henry Joy McCracken in 1997 and I painted a portrait of McCracken for the cover of the book. Charlie Haughey bought this painting from me in 1998 and it hung on the walls of his mansion in Kinsealy for eight years before he died in 2006. His estate put the painting up for auction and by pure luck I was alerted to the sale. I bought the painting back and kept it for two

years before giving it to Gerry Adams to mark his 60th birthday in October 2008. By funny coincidence I was born just a couple weeks before Gerry Adams and Prince Charles in 1948. The painting of Henry Joy McCracken was duly and appropriately hung on the wall of the Sinn Fein corridor of Dail Eireann. Since 1999 I have consistently supported Aengus O'Snodaigh in all his subsequent election campaigns. I have also backed Criona Ni Dalaigh in her election campaigns for Dublin City Council and I was delighted that she became the first Sinn Fein Lord Mayor of Dublin in time to mark the 1916 Easter Rising. I became firm friends with Aisling and Criona and the O'Dalaigh family including the late Sean O' Dalaigh who was a member of the Conrad Na Gaeilge branch in Inchicore.

The Orchard

The Orchard was a small sweet shop which had stood at Kilmainham Cross for more than a hundred years. It was renowned by people form all across the city as a gathering point for cyclists who set out in large groups on Sundays in the forties, fifties and sixties and often cycled say to Tullamore and back in the one day. It was also known by all who frequented the Phoenix Park of a Sunday afternoon as a place to stop and buy ice-cream or lemonade.

Sometime in the early seventies the proprietor Mr. Harrington died and his wife found it difficult to keep the shop going because of constant break-ins and robberies. The shop became derelict with briars and weeds growing out of it from every angle. The tourists from Kilmainham Gaol had to dodge briars and nettles as they passed it on their way to the local bus stop. I asked the Taoiseach Bertie Ahern to have it taken under compulsory purchase as one individual was attempting gain squatters rights on the premises. The local Inchicore and Kilmainham Development Project wanted it developed as a Tourist office or as a Heritage Centre. Dublin City Council duly succeeded in getting it under a CPO. However things did not turn out as we had hoped. No sooner had DCC got hold of it than they sold it to a private developer for 1.7 Million Euro. I had proposed that the site be cut back and planted with seating and monuments and flags and flower displays as would be befitting a site

that was in the foreground of Kilmainham Gaol. The site was designated Zone Z on the City Development Plan for recreation and amenity. The Council offered it for development for apartments of up to four stories high. I contacted Councilor Vincent Jackson who put forward a motion opposing the sale of the site. We had sufficient votes to stop the sale of the site but the City manager offered us a compromise saying that he would guarantee that any building that would be placed on the site would be sympathetic to the adjacent National Monuments, Kilmainham Gaol and The Royal Hospital . Sadly these were empty promises. Put not your faith in Princes or City managers. After two trips to An Bord Pleanala we were landed with what is now generally accepted as the ugliest building in Dublin on a site that was identified on the City Development Plan as "The Gateway To Inchicore."

The Shelbourne Hotel

So at Christmas in 1999 my brother Brian announced that he was going to New Mexico to live with the American Indians and leaving his job as a kitchen porter in the Shelbourne Hotel. As I had recently tired completely of working in the Printing and had accepted my third tranche of redundancy money I had a romantic idea that I could return to my carefree days of being a pageboy in the Royal Hibernain Hotel. The fact my brother had given in his notice enabled me to jump in and offer my services before the vacancy was even advertised. Thus I landed a job as a kitchen porter in the Shelbourne. There is quite a difference between being a pageboy and being a kitchen porter. The title might imply that you carry things around. Kitchen porters in the Shelboure were responsible for manning the pantry which was in effect a gigantic dish-washing machine. As such I was also obliged to man the |pot-wash" which required every pot, pan, vat, and large cooking vessel to be washed in three gigantic sinks by hand. Naturally we were also required to remove all waste food from the premises and this amounted to several tons per week. Again, the Shelbourne Hotel like the Royal Hibernian Hotel before it was a very beautiful hotel with an illustrious past having being used as a vantage point by British army snipers to shoot at the Volunteers in the Green in 1916 and where the first constitution was drawn up by Michael Collins after the Sinn Fein election victory in the 1918. However the glamour and glitz at the front of house wasn't matched by conditions in the back of the house. The Hotel was an amalgam of three Georgian houses facing onto St. Steven's Green and was very higgedly piggedly with stairs going every which way except sensible. There were five kitchens in the hotel and it was a damn difficult job to keep them all clean. The waitresses did their best to to keep the appearance of style at a high level at the front of house while chaos often reigned below stairs. I was moved to write a poem expressing this contradiction.

The Waitress

She catches glimpses
of eternal truth
criss-crossing the checker-board
of life
from Banquet Halls in splendour dipped
from gourmet meals
to refuse tips
through kitchens hot and basement's grot
down motley halls
to pastry chefs
past pantry's noise and dour pot-wash
avoiding spills and messy slips
round awkward chairs
and squeezing fits
down many stairs
up many lifts
till last she rests her sterling tray
and shakes her cloth
still shining white
and leaves behind the dull and grey
and steps into the
dazzling light.

© Michael O'Flanagan   February 2000

Beaumont Hospital

One of my jobs in the Shelbourne was to wheel out the bins. This sounds like a very innocuous chore. However there were no service lifts in the hotel and everything had to be carried up and down several stairs. For example, the ice-making machine was on the third floor and buckets of ice for the various lounges had to be carried down to cool the patrons drinks. There was also a banqueting kitchen on the first floor with only a very narrow stairs up and down to it. Unlike other kitchens where each individual meal was cooked and served to order in the banqueting kitchen meals were prepared in advance for up to one hundred guests. This required very large volumes of vegetables to be pealed, washed and chopped, cooked and laid out in a splendid display. It also meant that there was a huge amount of refuse created in the form of unwanted stalks, skins and leaves. These were then deposited in large wheelie bins which had to be wheeled down the stairs because there was no service lift. One day this task fell to me. Fell is the correct word. I pulled a wheelie bin weighing about a hundred-weight down the stairs and it broke loose and slammed me into the wall at the bottom of the stairs. As people are wont to do in such circumstances, I jumped up and congratulated myself on being still alive. I could still walk about and despite being quite numb I felt no pain. However after a week of two I began to stumble about as if I was constantly drunk. Everyone noticed it. I went to my doctor and he said he thought it was a virus. He ordered some blood tests and gaily announced that there was nothing wrong with me. However I insisted that he refer me to a consultant in St. James's Hospital. Because of my very unusual way of walking the consultant was convinced I had Mad Cow disease. This was all the rage at the time. He took me into hospital and carried out a range of tests including EEGs, lumber-punctures and finally an MRI scan. The scan showed that I had two burst discs in my neck at C3 and C4. These were protruding and impinging on my spinal chord and preventing the correct messages being transmitted from my brain to my legs and feet. This was why I had a funny walk. I needed neurosurgery and so I was transferred to Beaumont Hospital. I was put under the care of Mr. Young who immediately recognised that my condition could only have been caused by blunt force trauma. Apparently if was very common among Rugby players and he had dealt with several cases successfully. He asked me what had happened to my neck. I mentioned the wheelie bin incident and he was happy to confirm that that was the proximate cause. However Mr. Young played a lot of golf and had booked a golfing holiday while I was anxious to have my surgery as soon as possible as my condition was deteriorating and I might have ended up in a wheel-chair. He handed my case over

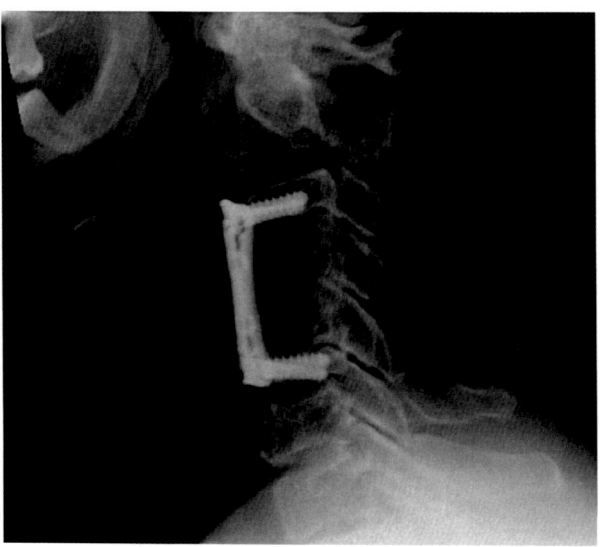

to Mr. Bolger newly arrived from London who was reputed to be one of the best neurosurgeons in Europe. A senior nurse in the hospital told me I had the best of both worlds with Mr. Young's diagnosis and Mr. Bolger's hands on skill. And so it turned out, Mr. Bolger's nine hour operation on me was a complete success. The four titanium screws he drilled into my neck have never slipped even after eighteen years. I was able to receive compensation for my accident from the Shelbourne Hotel with the assistance of my solicitor Ms Caoimhe Haughey who did an excellent job in establishing that a service lift should have been provided for the transport of wheelie bins from the banqueting kitchen to the ground floor. The Shelbourne Hotel has since been totally refurbished and no doubt all of these anomalies have been suitably adjusted.

The Kilmainham and Inchicore Heritage Group

In the wake of the debacle regarding the Orchard, Dublin City Council agreed to sponsor the establishment of a heritage group in the area. The Council had recently established local area development sections called IAPs meaning integrated area plans. The manager of the Kilmainham IAP was Gerry Folen and he called a meeting in Inchicore College to establish a new heritage group for the area. Approximately forty people attended the meeting and a host of idea's were put for developing and protecting the heritage of the area. A committee was set up to lead and organise a proper heritage group fitting to the historic nature of the area. Many of those who had been involved in the Inchicore and Kilmainham Development Project attended. Others had moved on to do different things and the idea of this new group was to concentrate on the historical and heritage aspects of the area. Councillor Michael Conaghan proposed himself as Chairman of the group and this was accepted by those present. I proposed myself a Secretary of the group and this was agreed by those present. Others who agreed to serve on the committee were Helen Scott, Councillor Catherine Byrne, Seosamh O Broin, Peter Keenahan, George Saunders, Phil McGibney and Ray McGovern It was agreed that the committee could meet in the

Kilmainham Office of Dublin City Council on the Sth. Circular Road. Meetings were held monthly and an ambitious plan was put

together to draw up maps, put up plaques and research and publish articles relevant to the history and heritage of the area. Shortly after the group was set up Michael Conaghan was elected Lord Mayor and for a time meetings were held in the Mansion House. Phil McGibney was a keen photographer and he took important photographs illustrating the heritage of the area. The first plaque erected by the group was on the house where the poet Michael

Hartnett who had lived on Emmet Road. Another plaque was put up on the Gymnasium of Richmond barracks to mark where Francis Ledwidge had given readings when he was stationed there in1915. During this period we had the unwavering support of Patricia

Tierney who worked in the area office in Kilmainham. She also gave enormous assistance when we put on a major heritage exhibition in the newly built Inchicore Sports Centre. The exhibition which was launched by Brush Shiels was composed of two hundred photographs specially enlarged for the occasion and reflecting the heritage of the area going back to the 1800s. It also featured recordings of oral histories of the area given by senior citizens who remembered Kilmainham and Inchicore from times long forgotten. Some aspects of the area's history were not universally appreciated by all the members. Namely the republican history of the area. Some wanted to concentrate on the architectural heritage of the area at the expense of marking the area's connection with the struggle for Independence or indeed the Trade Union connections with the area. All were agreed to put up a plaque to Joe Carr one of Ireland's most famous golfers who was born on Turvey Ave. Ray McGovern was very much to the fore in getting this plaque put up with the help of the Irish Golfing Union. However when it came to marking the significance of Emmet Hall on Emmet Road which was bought by Jim Larkin in 1913, not all of the members put their backs into it. I approached Jack O'Connor of SIPTU and he agreed to pay for two plaques to be put up on this important building. We held a ceremony to mark the erection of plaques in 2011 and we received maximum

cooperation from the owner of the premises Mr. Des McDonald. The significance of this building surpassed the man who purchased in 1913. It was involved in the Lockout in 1913 and the Easter Rebellion of 1916. Apart from being secretary in charge of minute taking and communications I became a near full time organiser for the group. So it was largely left up to me put on the three exhibitions in this Hall marking the Lockout, it's association with the Irish Citizen Army, the Irish Volunteers, Michael Mallin, his family and other notables such as Con Colbert. Mallin and Colbert were executed for their part in the Easter Rising. Mallin was living in Emmet Hall when he was executed and his family continued to live there until 1924. Sadly less than half of the members of the heritage group bothered to attend these exhibitions even though the exhibition marking the centenary of the Rising was on view for the whole month of May in 2016. Luckily people from outside the area had a better appreciation of the occasion and the building. Mr. Byran Dobson the anchor newsman from RTE agreed to launch the exhibition on the 4th of May 2016. The exhibition was attended by people from all over Ireland and was favourably reviewed in the local press at a time when the nation was marking the birth of Ireland's Independence.

Riposte

Three poets outside Aras An Uachtaran

In around the same time as we set up the The Inchicore Ledwidge Society I decided to launch a Poetry Broadsheet. I had had some success in winning a commendation from The Gerard Manly Hopkins poetry competition but it was extremely difficult for new writers to get published in Ireland. I had submitted a number of poems to Poetry Ireland without success. I got the idea from the newsletter I had been sending out from the Constitution Club. Working in the printing I was familiar with "impositions" that is the way multiple pages are arranged for printing so that they can be folded in order for the pages to read in sequence. An A4 sheet of paper can be folded so as to produce a brochure with six pages. Likewise I knew that an A3 sheet could be folded to produce a broadsheet with nine pages and this could also be wrapped into itself to make an envelope. This enabled me to produce a broadsheet containing twelve poems on both sides of the sheet but also leaving a blank square for an address label and a stamp. The idea was that the broadsheet could be put in the post and delivered to all the members of the publication on the same day and at the same time. It took some time to build up a mailing list and I had to subsidise the Broadsheet for a number of months until members had the confidence to join up and subscribe. The whole thing was possible at the outset because there was a Second Class post at the time whereby "unsealed letters" could be posted at a reduced rate. In order to drum up interest I included a celebrity free list which I published at the top of the Broadsheet beside the Masthead. Significantly nearly all of those who were included on the free list eventually sent in subscriptions and donations which boosted the circulation made the project viable. Also for a period of ten years Guinness gave us a small grant which was of great assistance and

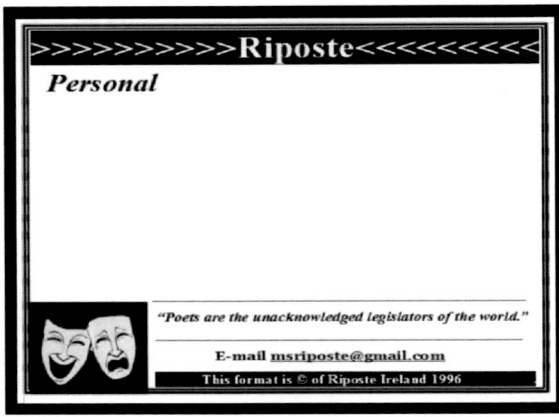

enhanced it's credibility among our subscribers. I called the broadsheet Riposte for two reasons. One it contained the word "post" in the middle of the title but more importantly it was intended to be a "riposte" to those in the establishment who kept a "closed shop" and shared out among themselves whatever support or opportunities were available to established writers provided they were already "In." New-comers could whistle. If you were "in" you were "in" and if you were not "in" you were not getting "in." Needless to say in the twenty years of it's existence Riposte never got a penny from Poetry Ireland or The Arts Council despite numerous applications. Nevertheless one hundred and ninety issues of Riposte were published featuring two hundred and forty seven poets from eleven different countries over a period of twenty years. Many poets had their first poem ever published in Riposte and went on to publish successful collections and gain fame in the wider literary world. Many friendships were forged via Riposte and it acted as a social hub long before social media dominated the land. The following commendations came from regular readers of Riposte."Congratulations on your broadsheet- I am delighted to see such a true and open forum, especially for new poets. Salute! " Paul Durcan "Good luck with the broadsheet, looking forward to seeing it." Paula Meehan "Full marks for design and ingenuity" Áine Miller "A terrific idea and very well presented" Michael Herron " I've become hooked on receiving my little "Pink and Blue" bundles." Noelle Vial "Best wishes with the broadsheet, keep them coming" MacDara Woods " Thank you Riposte, for your very unique contribution to my life." Daphne Kirkpatrick "I'm delighted with Riposte, it's not just for fancy poets" Michael Hartnett "It's very elegant, I love the layout." Brendan Kennelly "Well done to all involved in Riposte for their outstanding service to so many new poets" Tony Gregory TD. "I have enjoyed reading Riposte and hope that you continue the good work." Robert Ballagh "I congratulate the editor of Riposte, those of us who care about poetry salute your commitment." Desmond Egan "Riposte, Ireland's most talked about poetry publication." Liam O'Meara "Thank you for your poetry which I greatly enjoyed." Jeremy Paxman "Thank you for Riposte which you have sent to me since I became Minister. I, and my staff enjoy your publication and look forward to its arrival." Sile de Valera, Minister for Arts, Heritage and Gaeltacht. " Continued success with your fantastic work with filí agus baird na hEirann" An Taoiseach Bertie Ahern T.D. " I have a great love of Irish poetry and hope that Riposte will instil greater interest in changes in this field. I look forward to receiving further copies in the future." Mary McAleese Uachtarán Na hÉireann. Poets who had their poems published in Riposte had the satisfaction of knowing that those making the above commendations were reading their poems. Naturally when a poet saw a copy of the broadsheet dropping in through their letter box they would race to see if their poem had been included. I must remember many of Riposte's long-standing supporters who left the stage and went to their eternal rest such as Michael Hartnett, Jim Mitchell, Eamon MacThomáis, Thomás McGiolla, Tony Gregory, CJ Haughey, Warren O'Connell, Tommy Murray and Phyllis Eustace. I had to close up the Broadsheet in 2015 when the cost of postage rose to one Euro per item. The internet has now taken over in terms of the publication of poetry but those members of Riposte who have carefully kept a complete collection of Riposte issues have not only a piece of Irish literary history but a significant collection of philatelist's items.

The Inchicore Ledwidge Society

So having been a member of Syllables for a number of years and having come to understand the connection between the poet Francis Ledwidge and the area myself and Liam had the idea to establish The Inchicore Ledwidge Society. A friend of ours, Tom Macken had

a strong devotion to Ledwidge and he regaled us with stories about his Inchicore connection and it seemed natural that Ledwidge's association with Richmond Barracks should be celebrated by the people of the area. Liam set out to do a deep study of Ledwidge and his poems and we both studied his biography by Alice Curtayne. Most people knew of Ledwidge from his poem Thomas MacDonagh which had been on the school curriculum for years. Liam set out to collect Ledwidge's unpublished poems and discovered sixty six poems that had not been included either in Dunsany's collected

poems of Francis Ledwidge or in Curtaye's Complete Poems. We invited a number people knowledgeable about poetry who were interested in Ledwidge, and his connection with Inchciore to join our Society including Declan Collinge and Alison Maddock. We visited Slane, Ledwidge's home town and met with members of the Ledwidge Cottage committee who had been promoting the memory and work of Francis Ledwidge from as far back as his 50th Anniversary in 1967. We met with the Poet's nephew Joe Ledwidge and Ellie Vaughey's niece Mrs Pearl Baxter. Both members of the Cottage Committee they were delighted that a new association dedicated to Ledwidge was being formed in the Capital. We held an inaugural dinner in The Royal Hospital Kilmainham followed by a wreath-laying ceremony and poetry reading in The National War Memorial Park at Islandbridge on the 31st of July 1995. Our guests speakers included Pearl Baxter and the celebrated poet Michael Hartnett. Liam subsequently published a more complete collection of Ledwidge's poems in conjunction with Goldsmith Press. Later still he published several books on Ledwidge including a new biography, Ledwidge's prose under the title Legends of the Boyne and a short collection entitled the best of Francis Ledwidge. These books were published under my imprint Riposte Books. Meanwhile I acted as secretary of the Inchicore Ledwidge Society and we held a

Poetry Reading and wreath-Laying Ceremony in The national War Memorial park every year from 1995 up until 2018. On seven occasions The Lord Mayor of Dublin was our guest of honour reading a poem and laying the wreath. Our Society was twice hosted in Aras An Uachtran by both Mary McAleese and by Michael D. Higgins. Our signal year was 2017 which marked hundredth anniversary of the death of Francis Ledwidge in WWI. We held a week long exhibition in Richmond Barracks formally opened by Eamonn O Cuiv TD. and we had a Gala Poetry Reading in Kilmainham Gaol to mark the occasion. In 2016 we commissioned a sculpture of Francis Ledwidge to be displayed in Richmond Barracks marking his association with the Barracks where he trained as a soldier before going to war in 1915. Liam O'Meara wrote a play on the life of Francis Ledwidge which I produced and it was performed in the Patrick Pearse Theare in Pearse Street in 2013. The play was directed by veteran director Frank Allen and starred Tomas Gleeson, Ken Fletcher and Niamh Kavanagh. It ran for one week and it was widely applauded. The Play was videoed and may be viewed on Youtube. Our Society has been hugely successful coming up as it is now to being nearly a quarter of a century old and being recognised both in Ireland and abroad. Throughout that period we have worked in harmony with the Francis Ledwidge Cottage Committee in Slane. Many hundreds of Ledwidge enthusiasts have

Orla Martin, Mary Guckian Christine Broe, Me, Catherine Anne Cullen, Jean O'Brien and Mary Turley McGrath in Kilmainham Gaol 2017

enjoyed our Ledwidge Days every year and we always have reception in the Glen of Aherlow Pub in Kilmainham after the annual event. I persuaded Robert Ballagh to paint a portrait of Francis Ledwidge in 2012 and it became a very popular image and featured in many publications marking the poet's centenary.

St. Michael's Estate Regeneration Board

I first met Rita Fagan when a meeting was called in St. Michael's Parish Centre to discuss the newly announced EU structural funds for local development in 1988. As I had been dealing with these issues at the Constitution Club and had my own idea's on how local government should be reformed I attended and tried to make an impression in the local context. This was the first time I got a clear picture of the problems and difficulties that existed in the Inchicore area. Rita spoke at the meeting and explained that a task force had been set up to deal with problems that surrounded St. Michael's Estate. Apart from drug-dealing and squatting in some of the apartments there had been a number of suicides on the estate arising from the near impossibility of families having a norrnal life while living under these conditions. The meeting took place in a packed hall and a host of other grievances were voiced from other parts of the community resulting in some heated exchanges. The outcome of the meeting was to setup The Inchicore and Kilmainham Development Project. I worked very satisfactorily with Rita on this group and learned about the work herself and Sister Jo Kennedy were doing in the Family Resource Centre locally. Meanwhile Dublin City Council had carried out a poll among the residents of St.

Michael's Estate and it was decided to demolish the eight blocks of flats and replace them with regular two storey houses using extra land which had been acquired from Goldenbridge Convent. The

Rita Fagan protesting outside City Hall

work was to be carried out in phases and the residents were to be decanted into the newly built houses and the blocks knocked down gradually. The first phase went ahead without hitch but then the

Eilish Comerford handing out leaflets outside City Hall

Government changed policy and proposed a PPP a public, private, partnership whereby the Council would hand over the land to a Private Company and in return the company would deliver a portion of the apartments and some service buildings to the council. At first this was intended to be done without consultation with community but after substantial pressure from the community backed by local councillors the Government relented and set-up St. Michael's Regeneration Board. Throughout this period I fully supported The Regeneration Team which consisted of Eilish Comerford, Sister Jo Kennedy, Rita Fagan, Dr. John Bissett and a number of others.

Eadaoin Ni Clearaigh and Martin McGuinness in Richmond Barracks

I joined the board which met every month and included representatives from Dublin City Council and a number of local service providers including the Family Resource Centre, the Drugs Task Force, local Gardai, Local Empolyment Services, local residents and local Councillors. Finbar Flood was appointed Chairman with Eadaoin Ni Cleraigh acting as CEO and much work was done over three years in guiding the proposals for a new start under a PPP which would deliver not just a very beautiful replacement for the eight storey blocks that had failed but would deliver social regeneration into an area that had significant manifestations of deprivation and poverty. After three years of hard work a contract was signed with Bernard McNamara's Company to deliver a brand new future for Inchicore. It would have a new village centre with a civic centre, a new library and a wide range of styles of

Myself outside Anglo Irish Bank

housing and apartments. It would also have adequate green space playgrounds and sports facilities etc. Unfortunately within weeks of the contract being signed the economic collapse hit Ireland, McNamara went bankrupt and the whole plan went into the bin. The Board remained in position and I chaired a number of meetings over a year when we tried to get Dublin City Council to proceed with some aspects of the plan. Because the Government had no money and the Dublin City Council had no money this was no easy task. It required tremendous political pressure and Rita Fagan's Regeneration Team whipped up a storm which ultimately delivered seventy two houses and apartments in Thornton Heights . The re-development of the remainder of the fourteen acres of St. Michael's Estate is still in play as I write.

John Gallagher and Liberties Heritage

I first met John Gallagher at some of the commemoration events to mark the bi-centenary of the 1798 Rebellion. He organised several parades in the Liberties to mark the occasion. Being a Labour Councillor at first I was puzzled as to why he was so involved in

events that were primarily endorsed by those of a republican bent but I soon realised that it was his love for Liberties and it's connection to Robert Emmet's Rebellion that had him all fired up. His energy and organisational skills were immediately apparent and I was very impressed. Later I became better acquainted with John when I joined the The Regeneration Board for St. Michael's Estate.

He was a staunch supporter of the plans for it's re-development and never missed a meeting of the Board. By 2003 I was living on a disability pension after my accident in the Shelbourne and my operation in Beaumont. My occupational therapist recommended that I seek sheltered employment and John operated a number of Community Employment schemes and he offered me a position which enabled me to bolster my income a little. What was most

attractive about this was the nature of the scheme. It was a heritage research program calculated to gather together all the existing heritage and history of the liberties. This was done by the participants of the scheme researching individual aspects of a particular theme for a particular era or year. When I joined my task was to write a Local Dictionary of Biography including the names of all the famous characters who lived or been associated with the Kilmainham Inchicore area. This I did this most effectively and had nearly completed a four hundred page book when my hard-drive crashed and I lost four years work in a nano-second. However at the same time I wrote a short biography of John Gallagher himself and we launched this in Carmen's Hall in Francis Street with great celebrations. John ran Carmen's Hall with the co-operation of the

Nuns who had previously owned the building as a school and with support of St. Luke's parish. The centre was the heart of the Liberties community with every sort of activity taking place in the hall. They supplied free breakfasts to local children before school every morning. In the afternoon the elderly could have a dinner for a very modest fee. Scouts, girl-guides, marching bands and numerous local institutions had a home in Carmen's Hall. Books were launched there, films were shown and parties for the elderly were held there regularly. The biggest event of the year was the Liberties Heritage Exhibition. This amounted to about twenty large exhibition boards with hundreds of photographs and accompanying narratives usually on a single theme. Examples were in 2009 the exhibition

Mrs Fitzsimmons myself and Mrs Dunne at the Gunniess Exhibition

centred on the history of Guinness marking it's 250th anniversary in the area In 2010 I persuaded John to mark the 800th anniversary of the arrival of King John .in Dublin in 1210. This was a huge success but it marked my last year with the scheme as my health had deteriorated and I could not attend to the work as diligently as before. John Gallagher was one of the kindest men I have met in my seventy years on this earth. The work and dedication he gave to the liberties community can never be sufficiently recognised.

Richmond Barracks

Seosamh O Broin had spent sixty years collecting the history of the Inchicore area and he was a great repository of knowledge for the heritage group at all times. He was determined to have something done with Richmond Barracks which he considered to be central the significance of the area. Meanwhile Michael Conaghan had been interested in having the Railway Works at Inchicore developed as a museum. He was also pushing for Kilmainham Mill to be adapted and made accessible to locals and tourists alike. So two issues began to dominate the debates at the group meetings as to which should be the main focus of activity. Eventually it was agreed to establish two sub-groups, one to concentrate on Richmond Barracks and one to concentrate on Kilmainham Mill. It was thought that the Railway project would be a much longer fight. I decided to concentrate my efforts on Richmond Barracks. As our group had lost the valuable assistance of Patricia Tierney who had been moved from the Kilmainham office we now needed partners to advance a cause that required some professional skills. Luckily for us Eadaoin Ni Clearaigh, the CEO of St. Michael's Regeneration Board gave us the assistance we needed. She was able to setup meetings with the department of Heritage and we got several face to face meetings with John Kennedy, principle officer in that Department. This was in 2013 in the depths of the country's financial crisis. Naturally he was quick to point out that his Dept had no money to give out. However, Eadaoin secured a small grant to carry out a feasibility study on the possible value and cost of restoring Richmond Barracks. It's important to point out here that Richmond Barracks had actually been demolished in 1967 but there remained three small recreation rooms from the original building. These were the buildings we wanted restored. The Gymnasium in particular was significant

because the all the Rebels of 1916 had been held and court-martialed in this building. Eadaoin engaged a conservation Architect, Margaret Quinlan to carry out the feasibility study and she produced an excellent proposal. The Minister for heritage himself became very interested in the proposal but the Government still had no money. We put together a coalition of politicians and organisations to press for the proposal ranging from Sinn Fein to The British Legion. We were looking for a grant from the 1916 Commemoration allocation. With this coalition we were able to demonstrate cross party and cross community demand for the restoration of the barracks. It would symbolise the republican tradition as exemplified by the 1916 Rebels and the 108 years that the Barracks had been a British Army Garrison. As 2016 approached the Tánaiste Eamon Gilmore pressed the Taoiseach to back the proposal. Martin Mansergh who was on the advisory committee for the centenary commemoration also backed the plan. Finally it was agreed that the Barracks would be one of the main national projects to mark the centenary of the

Easter Risng. The assistant CEO of Dublin City Council was charged with bringing the proposal to fruition. As a member of the Ricmond Barracks Advisory Committe I urged that the project must include the replacement of the Cupola or light tower which was the one aspect of the Gymnasium that gave the site any visual distinction. This was eventually agreed and was achieved at a modest cost. I also pressed for a sculpture of the poet Francis Ledwidge to be installed in the barracks. The Inchicore Ledwidge Society raised the finance necessary to commission the sculpture and it has become an important exhibit within the complex. I invited Martin McGuinness to unveil the sculpture and he was delighted to do so. It was one of the last public engagements Martin carried out before he passed away later in 2016. He gave a moving speech and spoke with authority on the poetry of Francis Ledwidge which he knew very well as he was proud of Ledwidge's connection with Ebbrington Barracks in Derry. We were also joined on that day by Rosemary Yore, Chairperson of the Ledwidge Cottage Committee in Slane Co. Meath

The Great Book of Kilmainham

I had spent four years writing a Local Dictionary of Biography for Kilmainham and Inchicore . My computer crashed and I lost the entire book along with the electronic texts of all my other books. I was in no mood to go back and trace my steps to start the book all over again which was a pity because I had two hundred entries and when the new National Dictionary of Biography was published it only had twenty two entries for the area. Then Niall Stokes of Hot Press fame published a most beautiful book on the life of Philip Lynott. Because I had been invited to contribute to this book I received a free copy in the post. This was no paperback. It was an A4 size book with a beautiful cover. I was amazed at the quality of the production. It occurred to me that I could produce a similar size book of all the great historical writings about Kilmainham that I had been reading for four years. Millions of history books have been scanned by Google Books in conjunction with Stanford University. The best research on Irish History had been carried out by a number of historians in the 1800s. They made fascinating reading. Nobody is going to reproduce these works again especially as they are now available online. But all of these works are out of copyright. A large number of these books contain lots of history on Kilmainham which was an important topic of controversy throughout Irish History. I thought it would be nice to bring all of these histories together in a single book. I decided to call it the Great Book of Kilmainham and produce it in a fashion which would justify the hyperbole. Articles

included are (1) Saint Mhaighneann. (2) Kilmainham, Islandbridge and Inchigore. (3) The Knights Templar at Kilmainham. (4) Sale of Old Kilmainham Gaol. (5) Islandbridge Temperance Society (6) Dan Donnelly's Funeral at Kilmainham (7) The Priors of Kilmainham (8) (The Battle of Kilmainham (10) Calico Printing Works at Islandbridge (9) Charles Macklin Actor at Islandbridge (10) Report to The House of Lords on Conditions in Kilmainam Gaol (11) The Kilmainham Meeting 1820 with Cloncurry, O'Connell and Curran (12) The Lunatic Asylum at Islandbridge (13) Corruption Inquiry into Kilmainham Gaol I produced the book as a leather bound book with the title embossed in gold lettering. This book was A4 size but I subsequently had it reprinted as an A2 book which appears as size A1 when opened out. This exhibition copy is on view in the Inchicore Library on Emmet Road.

Paintings

Cill Mhaighneann 700 AD

I have considered myself to be a poet from the age of 17. However being a poet is not like a job. I worked in the printing for forty years. I was a printer every day for forty years. It's fifty three years since I wrote my first poem but I have not been a poet for fifty three

years. In truth you are only a poet when you are writing poetry and in my case that happens infrequently and most often it occurs to my surprise. I don't consider myself to be a painter either but that never happens by surprise. I have only made five paintings and in each case I was forced to do so by necessity. The painting of Henry Joy McCracken was necessitated by the need for a cover for my book. I had no skill at painting and it took me a year to complete the image. My method was simple. A thousand mistakes and a thousand

corrections. Having worked at the printing I understood very well how to mix colour. Achieving the correct colour is essential as the colours used must balance each other otherwise the finished work would have a discordant look. For me it was important to have an exact picture in my mind of the picture that I wanted to see when it was complete. There was no room for chance and no room for artistic expression. If the finished painting didn't tell the story that I wanted it to tell then it would be a total failure. That's why I couldn't work in oils or water colours . These require instant skill and cannot be corrected when they go wrong. Almost every time I put a brush to the canvas I went wrong. But that is the great saving of Acrylics. They dry quickly and you can paint over your mistakes constantly.

As stated above my first painting was Henry Joy McCracken. The only image I had was a black and white engraving from Dr. Madden's Lives of The United Irishmen. The image of Kilmainham Gaol in the background was a view from my bedroom window. My second painting was Kilmainham 700AD. This I needed it for my Great Book of Kilmainham. In our heritage group we had been

talking about Cill Mhaighneann being called after Saint Maighneann for years. He had lived in the seventh century but nobody had any idea what he looked like or what Kilmainham looked like 1300 years ago. I conjured up a montage of images relevant to the era and spent another year working on that. At the same time I made a painting of St. Maighneann himself by a similar manner. The painting of Cill Mhaighneann 700AD was unveiled and now hangs in Inchicore Library. I then determined to tackle the Orchard Shop which had been the bane of my life nearly twenty years before. There were only out of focus photographs of this building which had stood at Kilmainham Cross for over a hundred years. I wanted to re-capture the romance of this little shop which was still fixed in the memories of so many. When it was complete we had a grand unveiling in the Glen of Aherlow. It was unveiled by Brush Shiels and we were delighted that five of the Swift girls could be present for the occasion. The Swifts had owned this little shop for generations

Henry Joy Sculpture

Having been successful in getting the sculpture of Francis Ledwidge into Richmond Barracks my mind turned to my life long hero Henry

Joy McCracken. I approached the Bord of Governors of the Office of Public Works commonly referred to as the OPW. I proposed that the Heritage Group and the OPW would jointly commission a bust

of Henry Joy McCracken to be installed in Kilmainham Gaol where he had spent two years in 1776. The proposal was that the sculpture would unveiled on the anniversary of McCracken's 250th birthday on the 31st August 2017. I put forward this proposal in the middle of 2016 to give plenty of time for the bureaucracy to grind on. After a series of letters and appeals to the Minister for Heritage and the

bureaucrats of the OPW the answer remained a firm "No." By this time I was enamoured of the idea of having a sculpture of McCracken done in any case and went looking for a sculptor who could make a light-weight sculpture that I could carry around. I was lucky to find that one of Ireland's leading sculptors' Yoram Drori could make a light weight bronze sculpture. I went up to his studio I Castleblaney Co. Monaghan to view his work. I was completely amazed at the accuracy of the images he had created. He had just completed a number of figures relevant to the 1916 Rising. He had captured Patrick Pearse and James Connolly to perfection. He explained his method of working and I was satisfied that he was the man for the job. I asked him to do a bust of Henry Joy and to make it light enough for me to lift it unaided. By now I had gotten permission from the manager of Kilmainham Gaol to unveil the sculpture in the East wing of the Gaol on the clear understanding that I would remove it immediately after the ceremony. Yoram made a clay image of Henry Joy and I went back to view it prior to it being cast in bronze. I wasn't happy with the first image because he had

Henry Joy looking upwards whereas the most commonly known image of McCracken was of him looking down. I asked him to make adjustments and he agreed but I was nervous because like the Ledwidge sculpture before it I was not interested in any interpretation or artistic flourishes. My worries were unfounded, on my third visit to Castleblaney I was thrilled to see that Yoram had achieved perfection. He had produced a spectacular image of McCracken. I raised the finance from a number of local patrons including Vincent Stapleton and Luke Creighton. Dublin City Council also gave us a grant of 3,000 euro. I invited Robert Ballagh to unveil the sculpture as he had previously designed the stamp of Henry Joy McCracken back in 1998. I asked my old friend Andy Connolly to sing the ballad of Henry Joy at the launch. I also asked my close friend Brush Shiels to sing the Dying Rebel on the occasion. Ciara Scott of Kilmainham Gaol hosted the occasion and a wonderful event transpired. We got a write up in the Belfast newspaper The Irish News. This was followed up by coverage on

BBC Belfast. There was more interest in Belfast than in Dublin. As agreed I removed the sculpture from the Gaol after the event. But now what was I to do with the bust? I approached the newly appointed Minister for the OPW Boxer Moran. He was opening an

exhibition on Hunger-strikes in the Gaol. I gave him all the details and asked him to look into having the sculpture installed in the Gaol permanently. He was most co-operative and enthusiastic about the idea. After a couple of months I received a letter from a senior figure in the OPW saying we could have a temporary exhibition in the Gaol. It's hard to overturn the bureaucracy. However by that time I was in communication with The Linen hall Library in Belfast. They were delighted when I offered them the sculpture. They asked that we would postpone any unveiling in Belfast until the following May when they would be celebrating the 230th Anniversary of the opening of the Library. This suited us down to the ground. They put on a grand lecture and reception to mark the occasion. It was an unparalleled honour for me to speak and to unveil Henry Joy McCracken in The Linen Hall. Both in Kilmainham and in the Linen Hall I have felt as if I have put my hand back through time to shake hands with Henry Joy

Kilmainham Mill

The whole saga of Kilmainham Mill has gone on now for fifteen years. Michael Conaghan persuaded Dublin City Council to commission a conservation report on Kilmainham Mill back in 2002. At that time the Council was considering buying the mill. That plan fell through and the whole question of Kilmainham Mill has remained on the agenda of the Heritage Group since 2004. When the heritage group split into two sub-groups, one on Richmond Barracks and one on Kilmainham Mill, I chose to go with the Richmond Barracks group. With the success of the Richmond Barracks group I then turned my attention to the Kilmainham Mill question. Sadly the Kilmainham Mill sub-group had been less successful over the three years of it's existence. No progress had been made. In December 2016 I decided to launch a completely new campaign totally separate from the heritage group in the hope of bringing in new and fresh personnel to tackle this intractable issue. I booked the Patriot Inn for a public meeting and sent out hundreds of invitations by email. I got a thousand leaflets printed and myself and my wife Helena went about the local area delivering the leaflets over the course of a week. . The meeting a huge success with only fifty differing idea's as to what way to progress. Luckily having

spent a year chairing St. Michael's Regeneration Board I had the skill to curb the enthusiasm of the ten megalomaniacs present who wanted to take over the meeting and I prevented the gathering from

going off in ten different directions. Eventually it was agreed that our objective would be to get Dublin City Council to buy the Mill. How it was to be restored and what possible use would be made of it would be left to a later date as no agreement on that seemed remotely possible. We had sufficient difficulty in agreeing a strategy to go about getting the Council to buy the Mill. At first it was all about petitions and posters. Luckily as the months went by those attending the monthly meetings were whittled down to the rational and the dedicated. Michelle Heery took up the job as secretary which was no mean task considering the chaos encountered at some of the early meetings. Nevertheless she kept all those who expressed an interest constantly informed of the campaign's progress. Robert Foley commissioned a series of pull-up posters for display at events organised by the group. Raymond Lambert and Fintan Connolly and

Alison Maddock displays material produced by the Mill Photos :Damien Maddock

Maurice Coen organised a very successful facebook page. Vincent Stapleton hosted the group month after month in the Patriot Inn. Fintan also made an aerial video of the mill showing the surrounding landscape, the adjacent graveyard and it's luxuriant vegetation. Mary Waddell, Raymond, and Robert put together a presentation on the Mill for use in schools outlining the history of the mill, the course of the Camac river and the flora and fauna surrounding the mill. The group met with Dublin City Council officials on a number of occasions and were at all times assured that the Council still had the intention to purchase the Mill. The Mill was in receivership and a number of other impediments existed. The Council wanted vacant possession of the property but there was a sitting tenant on the site. This obstacle had existed for a number of years without resolution. I organised a private meeting between the assistant CEO of Dublin City Council and the sitting tenant and some kind of understanding was arrived at. Our group gave an oral presentation to the area committee of Dublin City Council. Several of the local politicians joined the campaign including Aengus O'Snodaigh TD, Joan Collins TD, Brid Smith TD, Cllr. Paul Hand, Cllr. Vincent Jackson, and Cllr. Tina McVeigh. I approached Damien Shine, the sitting

tenant and he agreed to give our group a guided tour of the Mill. We invited the Lord Mayor Mícheál Mac Donncha to join us on the tour and he fully endorsed our Campaign. Meanwhile Michelle, Robert, Mary and Raymond composed a brochure setting out the history and potential of the mill and Robert organised to have it printed. Luckily Vaughan Corrigan had organised a fund raiser for the Campaign which had been hugely successful and the money raised came in handy for the production of the brochure. I asked the newly elected Lord Mayor, Niall Ring if he would launch our brochure. He readily agreed, stressed his full support for our Campaign and offered us the Mansion House as avenue for the launch. At the same time I asked Mr. Brendan Kenny assistant CEO of Dublin City Council if he would fund a feasibility study for a possible viable use for the Mill. Mr. Kenny pointed out that such a feasibility had already been done and he provided us with a copy of it. We were suitably impressed by the in-depth detail of the study and it greatly re-assured us that the Council were serious about buying the Mill. I subsequently met with the City Manager, Mr, Owen Keegan and he assured me that the Council were hell bent on purchasing the Mill and that it would be developed as a completely heritage orientated project. As I write the Campaign is proceeding with determination, confidence and optimism that the long running saga of Kilmainham mill will be resolved soon.

Leo, Dots and Molly

Animals can be great companions. Myself and Lena have always had dogs even from when we got married first. Our first dog Ben was a child friendly dog and Ruadhan had great fun with him even as a toddler. Ciara's dog Abbey was a bit spiteful and used to drag down ornaments in the house whenever she was left alone if we were out. I never had a pet other than my pet hen Wilbur when I was five years old. I now have two dogs Dots and Leo. Dots is fourteen years old. When she was young and agile she could knock a bird down out of the air. She was faster than a flying bird. Leo is five years old and very regal. They are my best friends. Molly was not my cat. She was a neighbour's cat. She was twenty five years old and looked like she would live forever. She greeted tens of thousands of tourists coming out from Kilmainham Gaol every day as she sat at the bus stop opposite my house . Sadly she was killed by a passing car shortly after I took this photo.

The New Ireland Forum

The New Ireland Forum was set up by the Irish Government in 1983 in the wake of the Hunger Strikes in 1981 and as a result of the growing conflict the North of Ireland which was escalating at that time. Numerous written submissions were received from a wide range of organisations and a number of oral hearing were held in Dublin Castle where high profile delegations were interviewed and subjected to questioning on their submissions.

Below is a Question and Answer session with Michael O'Flanagan

The Chairman was Mr. Cathal O'Eachaigh, Chancellor of University College Galway. Also present were An Taoiseach Garrett Fitzgerald TD and Mr. Charles Haughey TD leader of the opposition.

Thursday 3rd November 1983

The next presentation is by Michael O'Flanagan.

Chairman : Mr. O'Flanagan is a printer by trade and is active in the trade union movement. In 1975, he joined Sinn Fein and for a period was PRO in Dublin for that organisation. He left Sinn Fein in 1982 after its federal policy was dropped from the constitution of that organisation. Today his presentation is on behalf of the Federalism and Peace Movement, an organisation that was formed in May 1983. To put the first series of questions to Mr. O'Flanagan I call on Senator James Dooge on behalf of Fine Gael.

Senator Dooge: Mr. O'Flanagan, you are very welcome here. We thank you for your submission and for forwarding to us the proposals of your movement. You indicate in your submission that you have changed your position radically, you have turned your back on all violence and tolerance of violence and now wish to bring forward a solution that you feel will achieve peace and stability without forcing the desires of the members of one tradition on the members of the other. would you tell the Forum briefly how this change in your thinking came about? what were the factors that influenced you in this significant change of position?

Mr. O'Flanagan: I believe that the operation of section 31 of the Broadcasting Act in the Republic has had an extraordinary effect within the Republican movement. It has frozen out the moderate leaders and allowed the hardline Republicans from the Six Counties to gain total dominance. The leaders of the Republican movement originally and up until the dropping of the federalism policy, as I would see it, were men who were guided by religious, moral or philosophical principles. Unfortunately, we have seen the arrival to power of the Northern Republicans. These people tend
to be soaked in bitterness and resentment as a result of the treatment they have been subjected to up there and they are often motivated by a naked desire for revenge. The operation of section 31 has in effect, brought these people to power. The result is that moral, religious and philosophical principles have been pushed into the background and the modern leaders of the movement appear to be operating on a totally pragmatic basis, that is that whatever advances the Republican cause is good and whatever inhibits the advance of the Republican cause is bad. I think morality should be brought back into the struggle. I reject violence and always have done as a means

of achieving any particular goal. However, it must be remembered that all individuals and all nations collectively have the right to defend themselves and that includes defence against foreign aggression. That right extends to the Nationalist people in the Six Counties as well as to the Nationalist people in the Twenty-six Counties.

Senator Dooge: you have put forward a proposal for a new Ulster. You have proposed that in your federal system there should be a return to a nine county province of Ulster. Do you think there is a real feeling of identity, an Ulsterism, that transcends the two communities in the Six Counties and crosses the Border to take in the three counties now in this State?

Mr. O'Flanagan: Since we published our policy I have received communications from people in East Belfast who have welcomed the proposals. I have also received communications from people in East Belfast who did not welcome them. They pointed out that the term "Ulstermen" is a term commonly used by Unionist people and rarely used by Nationalist people. However, this would not seem to be a bar, in my estimation, to Nationalist people assuming an Ulster identity. The people in Donegal, for example, clearly see themselves as Ulster people and ultimately the idea would be for all of the people there to assume a similar identity.

Senator Dooge: To turn from the sense of identity which, of course, any federal system would require to the details of the proposal you put forward, you suggest that in this two-tier structure the federal Government should be concerned with foreign affairs, with defence and with national finance. Would you not think that security would also need to have a federal aspect, not necessarily all matters of security and certainly not local community policing, but do you think that your system could work without security being at the federal level?

Mr. O'Flanagan: We believe that when communities were happy security would not be a great problem. The drive should be towards community-based police forces and that is how people should think. People should ultimately be able to defend themselves and to have control of the forces that they elect to defend them.

Senator Dooge: You have put forward a federal system rather than a confederal system in which, in the main, sovereignty would rest with the four provinces and then be transferred to the federal Government. Your proposal indicates that the power would be at the federal level and then devolved. would you be prepared to accept, in the interests of agreement, that the power would come from your four sections to the federal Government?

Mr. O'Flanagan: There are definitely two ethnic communities within the country. In fact many people would say there are more. We believe that federal government should be based on the unity and sovereignty of the Irish people as a whole and that the federal identity is something that even the Unionists could aspire to. The suggestion you are making that Dail Uladh could be outside of the federal solution would not appeal to us at all.

Senator Dooge: you propose it should be just a unicameral legislature. Your extended Ulster would contain 40 per cent of the population but it would only contain, on my reckoning, 32.5 per cent of the seats. Does this not involve an under representation of the people you are trying to attract?

Mr. O'Flanagan: All States in a federal system should be considered equal. This is the case in America, in Australia and in other places. Each State is considered to be of equal value in a federal system. That is what keeps them together.

Senator Dooge: Do you think it is essential in a solution, whether it be federal or confederal, that it should be based on four units? Do you think there could be a solution based on the two units that are there at the moment?

Mr. O'Flanagan: I do not think so. The treatment of the west of Ireland has been a deplorable thing within the Republic since independence was secured. I think Government should be devolved to the west of Ireland and to the south of Ireland.

Senator Dooge: You think that if you had a federal system and if the west of Ireland had more control over its policies and its finances it would be better off?

Mr O'Flanagan: It would be better off. People will say that the federal Parliament would not be ready to transfer finance to it. That is a tug-of-war that goes on in all federal states but it is overcome successfully.

Senator Dooge: An bhfuil ceist na teanga agus ait na teanga Gaeilge ina mbac do theacht le ch6ile an d6 thaobh den phobal sa Tuaisceart?

Mr. O'Flanagan: Ni chitear domsa go bhfuil aon dimheas i measc na Unionists do Ghaeilge. Ni doigh liom go bhfuil an Ghaeilge ina bac idir an di traidisiriin.

Chairman: Go raibh mait agat. we now pass to Mr. Eddie McGrady on behalf of the SDLP.

Mr. McGrady: I should like to endorse Senator Dooge's welcome to you. What, in your opinion, has been the effect of the campaign of violence on the aspiration towards Irish unity both in the North of Ireland and in the Republic of Ireland?

Mr O'Flanagan: I think there is a slight diminution of the aspiration among people in the Twenty-six Counties but I think that the resolve of the Nationalist people in the Six Counties has become stronger than ever. As to the progress towards unity itself and the oft-repeated phrase that violence puts off the day of unity, consideration should be given to the opinion that while the violence continues the question is being discussed. When the violence stops the question ceases to be discussed, as was the case for over 50 years.

Mr. McGrady: From what you have said it appears that you believe communities and individuals have the right to exercise violence in their own defence. What right do you think the Provisional IRA have to exercise violence in the North of Ireland without the consent of the people for whom they purport to act?

Mr. O'Flanagan: Each individual has the right to resist aggression from a foreign invader. The fact that the invader has been here for a long time does not interfere with that right. It is easy for people in the Twenty-six Counties to say the problem has been solved and we reject violence but the problem has not been solved for the Nationalist people in the Six Counties and they are being oppressed and they see themselves as being oppressed. They see their identity as being obliterated. They have the right to resist foreign aggression. They never accepted the settlement.

Mr. McGrady: The question I was posing was not whether an individual had the right to defend himself but whether an organisation had the right to arrogate to itself, without any authority, the right to use violence against another section of the community. How do you respond to that?

Mr. O'Flanagan: Up until the hunger strike, when attitudes changed drastically within the Republican movement, I would dispute that there was any direct antagonism within the Republican movement, I would dispute that there was any direct antagonism towards the Protestant or Unionist people as such. The aggression was directed against the British invader.

Mr. McGrady; And all the civilian deaths were simply innocent bystanders?

Mr. O'Flanagan: I will accept that civilian deaths occurred. It was never the policy of the movement at that time. It may be the policy of the republican movement at this time and this is something that appals me.

Mr. McGrady: Your submission says that you resigned from Sinn Fein when they dropped their federalism policy. Could you indicate why that happened? Did you feel that the movement then had ceased to have any consideration for the Protestant and or Unionist people in Northern Ireland at that time?

Mr. O'Flanagan: The Republican position has been that the Unionists and the Protestant people in the Six Counties are entitled to all the rights of every other citizen but their rights do not extend beyond that. There are always individuals within organisations who have motives other than the main motive of the organisation itself. The problem now is that the hard-line leadership have gained control of the Republican movement with the aid of outside forces - section 31 is a good example - and the moderate leadership has been frozen out.

Mr. McGrady: Do you see any provision or concession within the present policy of Sinn Fein to the accommodation of a different opinion within Northern Ireland or within Ireland?

Mr. O'Flanagan: So long as the current leadership of the Republican movement hold sway, i.e., people who are steeped in bitterness and resentment, it is possible that they will disregard the
Unionist position.

Mr. McGrady: You have described these leaders as men of bitterness, full of revenge, etc. These are the people who want to take over the leadership of the community that they are purporting to represent. Is that your opinion of the present position?

Mr. O'Flanagan: This is the danger but you must realise that the Nationalist people have also become bitter and resentful and they have shown their support for these men. The bitterness may extend throughout the community. It is a danger that the Forum and all political parties, North and South, must realise might come to fruition.

Mr. McGrady: What prerequisites do you consider necessary in order to achieve the agreement of the Unionist or Protestant community for your propositions?

Mr. O'Flanagan: So long as they wish to remain on the island of Ireland they should give their allegiance to a sovereign parliament, a federal parliament. This would not interfere with their beliefs, their traditions or their rights.

Mr. McGrady: In regard to Dail Uladh, with whatever counties it contained – six to ten and a half you mentioned – you state they would have a majority in any of those projections. Do you consider that majority rule would be a return to what was there pre-Stormont or do you see them having a new vision in that concept?

Mr. O'Flanagan: I see them having a new vision and I consider that the British guarantee to the Unionists is probably one of the most fundamental problems. So long as the British remain in Ireland the problem remains.

Mr. McGrady: What guarantee or series of guarantees would have to be made to the minority in that new division you speak of that would prevent a recurrence of what happened between the twenties and the seventies? What would have changed to make this more workable?

Mr. Q'Flanagan: The actual federal arrangements would have a balancing and checking effect on the situation in Dail Uladh, or the Northern parliament. People in the rest of Ireland are entitled at this point to ask whether the Northern Nationalists are being pandered to too much.

Mr. McGrady: Your map shows a considerable number of people who are now citizens of the Republic of Ireland who would be transferred into the new Dail Uladh. What do you think their reactions would be to being put in under what would then be Unionist domination?

Mr. O'Flanagan: Maybe not favourable but in the national interest -

Mr. McGrady: But is that not a problem?

Mr. Q'Flanagan: It might pose a problem but there are many problems posed by all solutions. In the national interest many things have to be carried out which are not appealing to individual communities.

Mr. McGrady: Your series of propositions have to be sold in another quarter, to the British Government, assuming that they were acceptable to the people of Ireland. What sort of reasoning would you use to indicate to the British Government that this was a desirable way forward?

Mr. O'Flanagan: First of all, I would have to point out that the British Government have no business being here in the first place. After that I would say that the cost of security to the British Government would be greatly reduced. Indeed, the cost of security in Ireland as a whole would be greatly reduced.

Mr. McGrady: There is not much difference from the British point of view between having a unitary Ireland or a federal Ireland if they are got out. You only mention the time element in the last page of your submission. The question I am posing is: how and when for British withdrawal?

Mr. O'Flanagan: The first move would be for the British Government to declare openly its intention to withdraw from Ireland. As regards the time scale it would not have to be particularly urgent, but it would not want to be too long either. Various television programmes have put about the idea that Ireland will be united within 100 years, so why worry? People took this attitude when the Treaty was signed. The result of this attitude has been violence throughout the decades.

Mr. McGrady: I have been asking you how do you persuade the British because your original premise, before you resigned, was that violence could be the means of persuading the British to withdraw. That is rejected in your paper and in your comments, so what is the method you would use to carry out this persuasion?

Mr. O'Flanagan: This Forum is a good example of one of the methods that can be used, but the Irish people as a whole should show by their voting patterns that that is the way they wish the situation to be resolved. Through international Fora of course as well.

Mr. McGrady: That is a pleasant note to end on.

Chairman: Now we pass to Deputy Frank Prendergast on behalf of the Labour Party.

Deputy Prendergast: I, too, should like to welcome you and to thank you for coming to us. Could you let us have some idea as to what kind of support your organisation or your political philosophy enjoys?

Mr. O'Flanagan: There has already been a submission made to this Forum by Mr. Desmond Fennell who is broadly of the opinion that a federal solution is a desirable one. There has been a submission made to the Forum by Mr. John Robb in similar vein and by Sean McBride. The probiem that our organisation finds at this time is that people within the Republican movement who support us decline to join us for one reason and people outside the Republican movement decline to join us for the opposite reason.

Deputy Prendergast: I presume it would be the intention of your organisation to consult the people of Donegal, Cavan and Monaghan in order to set up Dail Uladh as you envisage it. Is there not a lot of unreal expectation in the sense that if they rejected that proposal where then would your organisation stand?

Mr. O'Flanagan: lt would be our opinion that we should consult the people of Ireland as to whether this is acceptable and not consult individual counties as to whether they would like to opt in or out of a particular solution. This is one of the reasons we are in the situation we are in.

Deputy Prendergast: But, with great respect, is there not a lack of realism in some of the scenarios you posed? For instance, that the British would go, that three counties would go into a Unionist North and that the Unionists would have a new view, namely, that they would not fight?

Mr. O'Flanagan: I do not think there is any lack of realism. Once the British are removed from Ireland or leave Ireland the situation will be drastically changed and everybody's views of Ireland will alter considerably, probably even on the Nationalist side.

Deputy Prendergast: How would you reply to the suggestion that your proposed names - Dail Uladh, Dail Laighean and so on - would be insensitive and would be a cause of grave offence to the Unionist people?

Mr. O'Flanagan: Sirnply because they are in the Irish language?

Deputy Prendergast: Yes.

Mr. O'Flanagan: I never felt that the Irish language was a great barrier between the two traditions. Many eminent Irish scholars have been of other persuasions.

Deputy Prendergast: I think you would agree that they were very much in the minority rather than the majority and we have to deal with Realpolitik, the facts of life. We have to address ourselves to the vast bastion of opposition to the concept of a united or a federal Ireland. Is that not the reality of the situation?

Mr. O'Flanagan: I would not think that is the reality.

Deputy Prendergast: You speak about four levels of Government structure. Would you not agree that this would not only be unwieldly but would militate economically against the likelihood of such a proposal being adopted, that it would be a very costly type of structure for the taxpayer?

Mr. O'Flanagan: The cost of it is one thing, but whether it would be unwieldly is another. We believe that the more tiers of Government there are the better the people are protected from possible dictatorships and take-overs from the right or the left.

Deputy Prendergast: You say in your letter requesting an oral submission that many things have happened since the hunger strike at Long Kesh. Could you identify what these things are and how you could see the importance of this Forum?

Mr. O'Flanagan: The Republicans have become more hardline and bitter in their attitude, possibly because they did not get the support they expected from the people in the Twenty-six Counties for the sacrifices that were being made by the hunger strikers.

Deputy Prendergast: Does that not open up the question of your philosophy, while you might be opposed to violence as a principle? Does it not also highlight the fact that violence as a strategy has failed? As the Reverend McDowell has already said, not alone has it failed to diminish the opposition of the Unionists but instead has hardened their stance? It has also undoubtedly alienated or diminished the support of the vast majority of the people in the Twenty-six counties for what would be called the Republican movement in the North.

Mr. O'Flanagan: I do not take your point that it has alienated vast majority of the people in the Twenty-six counties from Republicans in the North. There has been a diminution in amount of support but not a vast diminution in that support.

Deputy Prendergast: Is that not a recognition that violence as a strategy has failed?

Mr. O'Flanagan: This is a myth that is perpetrated. All states come into being through violence, albeit the legitimate violence of the masses of the people, and all states maintain their independence by violence or the threat of violence. That is why the Republic has a standing army. It is a myth to say that violence always fails. The question is: can violence be restricted by moral forces?

Deputy Prendergast: You are speaking on a generalisation. I am confining myself to a particularisation, that in the particular with which we are concerned it has failed so far to achieve anything.

Mr. O'Flanagan: There are people of the opinion that this Forum is sitting today because of the violence in the North.

Deputly Prendergast: You say that the Northern Unionists enjoy only second class citizenship in the United Kingdom. Could you expand on that?

Mr. O'Flanagan: That is correct. Their representation does not entitle them to any great say in the government of the United Kingdom.

Deputy Prendergast: How do you think the Unionist people in the North could be induced to come into the type of overall political arrangement we would all hope for?

Mr. O'Flanagan: If the proposals are acceptable enough, and I believe these proposals are acceptable, they might be induced but, at the end of the day, it is not simply a question of inducing the Unionists into a United Ireland. The fact is that as people living on this island they have a duty to take part and to come in.

Deputy Prendergast: You say that conditions might be brought about that would make it attractive for them. Can I bring you back to a proposal made by Reverend McDowell, namely, that Irish should be taken out of the curriculum of national schools, that it has militated against the interests of some children? Would you see that as being an acceptable pre-condition, among others,
for the overall unity or federalisation of the whole country?

Mr. O'Flanagan: That would be a matter for the provincial parliaments. It might be possible for regions to have Irish in and other regions to have it out, just as it might be possible for one of the provincial parliaments to allow for divorce and another not to allow for it.

Deputy Prendergast: You say that all political prisoners should be freed. Surely this would not be acceptable to the Unionists?

Mr. Q'Flanagan: What is the life span of any prisoner? It may be unacceptable in the short term but all the prisoners would eventually die and they would not be in prison anyway.

Chairman: Thank You, Deputy Prendergast. Finally, we will have Deputy MacSharry on behalf of Fianna Fail.

Deputy MacSharry: You are welcome, Mr. O'Flanagan. Some of my points have already been touched on. If federalism is to have any point does it not mean effectively re-establishing Protestant control over the Six Counties albeit within an all-Ireland state and would they, under such a system, not expect to have an entirely free hand? Is this not a reason why the Nationalist community have tended to move against the federal solution?

Mr. O'Flanagan: I agree that is a danger. It is a threat that is posed. I believe that our system proposes balances and checks which would militate against such a regime coming into power. I repeat the opinion that as the Unionist population in- the Six counties do not have the right to a veto on the ultimate destiny of Ireland neither have the Nationalist population in the Six Counties a veto on the ultimate destiny of Ireland.

Deputy MacSharry: In practical terms is it not unrealistic to expect the Ulster counties inside the Republic to rejoin the rest of Ulster and submit themselves to protestant majority?

Mr O'Flanagan: I do not think the Ulster counties within the Republic have a veto either.

Deputy MacSharry: on the one hand, you say the attraction of your proposals is devolving power and, on the other hand, you say where certain counties should go and how they should be governed

Mr. O'Flanagan: They still would have power over day-to-day affairs, community policing etc., within their province. The people would have a genuine democratic say in the running of their province but no individual county should have the right to veto the ultimate destiny of Ireland.

Deputy MacSharry: would you accept that federal systems can create great practical difficulties and often conflict with regard to the division of powers and revenues between the federal and the subordinate parliaments?

Mr. O'Flanagan: I would accept that and I think it is one of the prices that has to be paid for genuine democracy.

Deputy MacSharry: Do you believe that Nationalist politicians would have any interest in attending a subordinate Stormont Parliament following the establishment of Irish unity?

Mr. O'Flanagan: There may be reluctance in the present situation to such a development but with British withdrawal from Ireland all present perceptions will be altered'

Chairman: Thank you, Deputy MacSharry, and thank you, Mr O'Flanagan for sharing your views and those of your colleagues Mr. O'Mahony, of the Federalism and Peace Movement, with us.

The Forum will now adjourn until 2.30 when it will reconvene in private session.